Translator Self-Training Italian

Practical Course in Technical Translation

Morry Sofer

Schreiber Publishing
Rockville, Maryland

Second Printing

Library of Congress Control Number: 2002105646
ISBN 1-887563-73-3

Printed in the U.S.A. by Schreiber Publishing, PO Box 4193, Rockville, Maryland 20849
www.schreiberpublishing.com

Preface

This practical course is for anyone who would like to pursue technical translation in Italian and English, in such areas as legal, medical, financial or other kinds of non-literary documents (literary translation is a different discipline from technical).

The course is based on the practical experience of a major translation company which has been translating routinely and successfully Italian-into-English and English-into-Italian documents in all technical areas for almost twenty years. The assignments in this book are taken from real-life documents which were translated by this company, with names and other information changed in some cases to protect proprietary information.

This book grew out of a correspondence course offered about ten years ago, which became a three-ring binder program for translator's self-training five years ago. During those five years, hundreds of translators have used this program each year, and many have offered unsolicited praise for this program, letting us know that it has improved their translation skills, and in more than a few cases helped the user pass accreditation or certification tests for such organizations as the American Translators Association (ATA).

Nothing sharpens translation skills more than the actual act of translating. But one needs an entry point, either into the technical translation field in general, or into new areas of translation, if one has already been doing one kind of technical translation, such as legal. This course provides the entry point.

We at Schreiber Publishing take a personal interest in translators in all languages and subjects, and are always happy to hear from you.

Enjoy the course!

Morry Sofer

Table of Contents

SECTION 1. GENERAL

INTRODUCTION

Welcome to the **Translator Self-Training / Italian**. We are very pleased you selected this program, which has been in use since 1990. It has helped aspiring translators around the country get their start in this exciting field, while assisting practicing translators in improving their translation skills. Translation is one of the fastest growing professions in today's world, as different languages and cultures are coming closer together every day. Whether you wish to pursue translation full-time or as a sideline, you will find it to be a highly challenging and quite profitable occupation. The purpose of the following exercises is to help you improve your skills as a translator of Italian and English.

This program is designed to help you work at your own pace and gain experience through translation practice assignments. These assignments, excerpted from actual translation jobs, were selected to help you determine your own level of comfort and expertise, so that you may go on from there to choose the type of translation work you may like to pursue.

To derive the maximum benefit from these texts, you should carefully read the General Comments, the guidelines, and the specific notes which discuss each assignment. Every comment and every guideline represents years of experience in professional translation work. By carefully following this program, you will be able to achieve *in just a few days* what has taken others years to learn. You will be guided through many of the pitfalls of translation, taught how to avoid them, shown shortcuts in accomplishing a complex piece of translation work, and be given the benefit of comments designed to show you how to produce a translation acceptable to major clients such as government, industry, the legal world, and many more.

Before you read further, we strongly urge you to read Appendix A: Requisites for Professional Translators, and Appendix B: Translation Techniques.

The above-listed Appendices will give you a good overview on how translation work is to be approached and practiced, and how to position yourself in the translation market. Try to keep the contents of these two sections in mind as you translate the following assignments.

You are presented with four different texts, which, for most people, represent an increasing level of difficulty (although if you happen to be a lawyer, for example, it is possible that you will find the second assignment the easiest of the four). They are:

1. **General**
2. **Legal**
3. **Chemical/Medical**
4. **Business/Finance**

At a minimum, you may want to do the first and second assignments. Those two represent a vast body of material which is being translated in the United States on a regular basis, but which does not require a highly specialized vocabulary or technical background. The third assignment requires access to chemical and medical terminology, which can be managed by any intelligent translator. The fourth assignment should be approached with caution. Here one must have an understanding of the world of finance, which not all of us do. For your own self-assessment, you may want to try it (since we provide you with the translation, you can compare the results and see for yourself how you did). But if you find it too difficult, don't be discouraged. It is clearly not for everyone.

We hope you enjoy working with these texts, and we urge you to please be patient with yourself. One does not become an accomplished translator overnight. To learn, one must make mistakes. If your heart is in it, and if you love the challenge of working with two languages you happen to know well, then you are sure to get a great deal out of this program.

A Word about Italian Translation

The volume of Italian translation in the English-speaking world is not nearly as large as, say, German or Spanish. Nevertheless, Italian is one of the world's major languages, and there is hardly a field of human endeavor where Italian influence has not been felt. This is true of everything from the fine arts to science and technology, from fashion to high tech, and other fields too many to enumerate in this small space. Whether or not one should pursue a full-time career as an Italian translator in the English-speaking world is hard to say. Certainly there is always a need for Italian freelancers, if only on a part-time basis, and there are indeed people who have successfully pursued full-time careers as Italian translators in places like England and the U.S. But clearly their numbers are not legion. As a general rule, if one happens to know Italian and has a flair for translation, it is certainly worthwhile to sharpen one's translation skills. If, on the other hand, one chooses to major in Italian in an American college or university with a view to making Italian translation a career, one should first examine the range of opportunities.

We would be remiss not to mention at this point that Italians have always excelled in the field of translation. Italian lexicography is excellent, and the practitioner of English-Italian translation has the great advantage of outstanding general and technical dictionaries and references. The kinship between the Italian language and the rest of Western culture, and the distinction of this language as arguably the most beautiful of European languages, make the task of Italian translation a unique challenge and a delight.

The following comments are offered with two purposes in mind: the immediate purpose is to help you with the assignments. The long-term purpose is to serve as reference material for actual translation work. Keep them for future use.

A reminder:

The "source language" is the language you translate from.

The "target language" is the language you translate into.

Every language has its own "personality," so to speak. When you translate, pretend you are two different persons - an "Italian Person" and an "English Person." The Italian Person reads the original Italian text, and becomes familiar with it. The Italian Person then turns to the English Person, and says to him/her, "Okay, now it's your turn to say the same thing your way." Now the English Person takes over, and starts writing the same text in English. You will be constantly switching back and forth between the Italian Person and the English Person, as the first checks the Italian word, phrase, sentence structure, and then the second thinks in English and comes up with the right equivalents. Here are some of the main language issues you will have to deal with:

Clarity

We each have our own personal style of expressing ourselves - in any language. Some people make their point clearly and succinctly, while others use more words than necessary, including esoteric words, to make their point. The same holds true in translation. You can translate the phrase "To call a spade a spade" as *"Dire pane al pane e vino al vino"* or you could also translate it correctly into the Italian equivalent of "One should always speak forthrightly and call things by their proper name." In the first instance, only six words were used; in the second, twelve. Most of the time, the first type of translation is better, because it is simpler and more readily understandable. Make it your point to pursue simplicity whenever possible.

Consistency

Most of the time, if you start out translating the word "house" as "*casa*," stick to "*casa*," and don't start suddenly shifting to "*edifizio*," or vice versa. The reader may become confused, wondering why the word suddenly changed. Generally in Italian, *edifizio* is bigger than *casa*, and one may wonder whether the dimensions of that particular structure might have changed. If you are familiar with word-processing you know how easy it is to do a "global search and replace" throughout the text, so that if halfway into the document you decide that "*edifizio*" is better than "*casa*," then go back to the beginning and do a global change, replacing the word "*casa*" with "*edifizio*."

Sentence Structure

It is difficult, yet very important, to ensure that sentence structure is correct and makes sense, yet still retains the flavor of the original text, particularly if this is written in a flowery, elaborate, or otherwise unique style. This fine line is achieved mainly through practice, but it is definitely helpful to read the original several times before even beginning the translation process in order to gain a good idea of the author's style.

It is not necessary to follow the structure of a sentence literally. A run-on sentence which may make sense in one language may not make sense in the other, and therefore should be divided into two sentences (or more). The converse is also true. You should also avoid being too literal when it comes to word order, or your text will sound stilted, awkward, and artificial. You will need to rely on your own good writing skills in determining the most sensible word order and punctuation so that your translation flows smoothly.

Format

Format should be followed as closely as possible. Ideally, every page of translation should look exactly like the corresponding page of the original, except, of course, for the language. There is a very practical reason for this. It helps the reader, who may or may not know the source language, compare the two texts, make sure all the parts are there, and check a particular word or phrase in the source text. This, however, is not always possible, since a page of translation at times is longer than the same page in the source language. Nevertheless, every effort should be made to keep the format as similar as possible to the original.

Terminology

The use of the right terminology is critical in any translation, especially in any technical subject. Here the right kind of dictionaries and reference literature becomes very critical. Keep in mind, however, that dictionaries, no matter how good, are never complete, and do not provide all the answers. The other source of information is people who work in the field the particular translation covers. Their input is often more valuable than that of the dictionary, since they are the ones who work in the field and represent the potential readers of your translation.

The first thing to keep in mind about terminology - as was discussed before - is consistency. If you translate a word a certain way, do not change in the middle of the text to another synonym of the same word, even though it may be accurate. This will throw the reader off. The second thing is to make sure you are using the right terms, rather than trying to approximate them. Keep a list of those terms to maintain consistency throughout the document, and also for future use. If you continue to translate in the same technical field, these lists will become your most valuable translation tool.

Numbers

The use of commas and periods is reversed in numbers over 1000 (1,000 in English becomes 1.000 in Italian), and in decimals (0.5 in English, becomes 0,5 in Italian). This is one example of cultural differences which must be closely observed.

Punctuation

Quotation marks are appropriate in English, but this is not always so in Italian. Punctuation in general is not always used in the same places. These are just a few examples of how even a highly accurate translation will not always mirror its original text. You will often be called upon to be the judge, which involves a combination of excellent writing skills, knowledge of rules of grammar and punctuation, plus common sense.

Errors in the Source Text

Sometimes you will find that the original has errors, such as a misspelling where it is clear by the context that the author intended to say "uno" and not "un," or the sequence in a series of numbered clauses is wrong, or a name that has been in upper case letters suddenly appears as lower case for no apparent reason. You can do a number of things in situations such as these. You can go ahead and make the correction and leave it at that. You can translate the text as is, and use the term [sic] after the error, to alert the reader. Or you can make a translator's note on a separate sheet of paper. Ultimately, the client will have to decide what to do with it.

Untranslatable Words or Terms

You may run into a word, a term or a phrase which cannot be translated, or which should be left in the original language (such as, for instance, "rock-and-roll"). If there is a need to explain it, it can be done in a footnote or in parentheses (or brackets, which makes it clearer that the bracketed text is not part of the original) following the word. As a general rule, however, it is best not to burden your translation with footnotes or parenthetic or bracketed text.

In Conclusion

The above notes are by no means exhaustive. They do not cover all the issues facing a translator. Language is not mathematics. Keep this in mind, and do the best translation job you possibly can.

GUIDELINES FOR TRANSLATING THE ASSIGNMENTS

1. We are providing you with an Italian text and an English translation of that same text. Pretend you don't have the English translation. If you read it before you do the assignment, you will not be able to do an honest job, and you will not derive the benefit of learning from your own mistakes.

2. Read the Italian text once for general comprehension. Underline any difficult words or passages.

3. As you start the translation process by reading the text for the first time (see 2., above), keep track of time, so that when you finish you will know how long it took you to translate the text. This is very critical, because you want to increase your translation speed as you go along. The rule is simple: The more words you translate per hour, the more money you will make. A very low hourly word-count can earn you less than minimum wage, which is not at all desirable. (Note: The hours indicated at the top right hand corner for each assignment include two numbers. The first is for beginners while the second number is for an experienced translator. Therefore, an assignment that would take a beginner 5-7 hours to complete might take an experienced translator 2 hours. The timeframe includes research, draft, and final copy.)

4. Read it again. This time make a list of difficult words, and make any notes regarding things you need to clarify about the text (e.g., look up something in an encyclopedia to better understand some concept or piece of information).

5. Try to determine which dictionaries and reference books you need for this assignment, get hold of them, and keep them nearby.

6. Now you are ready to start translating. Preferably, you will be using a computer. If this is too intimidating, write it out the first time. It will take longer, but you will have more time to think. Remember, your objective is to translate on computer, not in longhand. These days, if you want to earn money translating, you have to submit text on disk. There are hardly any exceptions to this requirement.

7. Do a draft translation. Go over the draft. Do the best you can to make the English sound like good, clear, correct English, which does not sound like Italian, and does not retain any Italian forms in either style, format, or any technical points. Be sure you did not omit anything. Ask yourself if you succeeded in conveying the correct sense of every idea and every word in the source text. Be sure you are comfortable with every single word you chose in English, and that you have no doubts or hesitations. If, after all this, you do have some questions, do not worry. No one expects you to do perfect work the first time around. You will do better next time.

8. Now that you have accomplished your translation, figure out the time it took you to reach your final version (including all the previous steps - namely, first reading, research, draft, and final copy).

9. Make a list of the words, passages, and concepts in the text where you encountered difficulty, and keep for future reference. This kind of record keeping will help you improve your performance, and serve as a reminder not to repeat the same mistake twice.

10. Print out your corrected and edited text.

GUIDELINES FOR SELF-EVALUATION

1. Turn to the English translation in Section 3, and compare it to yours. Next read the notes concerning the pitfalls and salient points of this text very carefully, and see how they compare to your own experience with the text. They may not necessarily coincide with everything you experienced personally, but they do provide you with some tips on the do's and don'ts of technical translation.

2. The most important thing for you to keep in mind as you compare your translation to the one in Section 3, is that there is no one absolutely correct way of translating a text. Many words can be translated in more than one way. Many sentences can be structured in more than one way. Many ideas can be conveyed in different words. In fact, your translation may turn out to be just as good, and in some spots even better than the one in the book.

3. Keep track of the shortcomings of your translation. The areas you are interested in are the following:

   Omissions - did you fail to translate any particular word or phrase, or even paragraph?

   Format - does your format follow the original (breaking into paragraphs, for instance)?

   Mistranslations - did you mistranslate any particular word?

   Unknown words - were there any words you were not able to translate?

   Meaning - did you miss the meaning of any particular phrase or sentence?

   Spelling - did you misspell a word?

   Grammar - did you make any grammatical mistakes?

   Punctuation - did you mispunctuate or miss any punctuation marks?

   Clarity - did you fail to clearly convey the meaning of any particular part of the text?

   Consistency - did you call something by one name, and then by another without good reason?

Cognates - were you "tripped" by a word in the source text, whereby you mistranslated it because it looked the same, though it changes meaning in the target language (for instance, the word "actual" exists in both English and Italian, but means two different things)?

Style - are you satisfied with the way your translation reflects the style of the original (for example, the original is written in a clear, direct style, while the translation sounds more complex and indirect)?

These are some of the questions you have to ask yourself. As you go on to translate other texts, always keep these questions in mind as you self-assess your translation. By improving your performance in the above areas, you are on your way to becoming an accomplished translator.

Part One

Translation: Italian into English

4-6/2 hours

ASSIGNMENT 1 - GENERAL

Bill apre le Gates di Internet

di LUCA DE BIASE

"Bill Gates è il più entusiasmante imprenditore del secolo" spara Jack Welch, capo della General Electric. "La Microsoft è il maggiore potere economico degli Stati Uniti" avverte Eric Schmidt, manager della Sun Microsystems. "La Microsoft sarà un problema politico prioritario per i prossimi 20 anni" prevede Mitchell Kapor, fondatore della Lotus.

William Henry Gates III. Bill. Giano bifronte dell'industria americana. Ponte tra passato dei pc e futuro della società dell'informazione. Davide negli anni Ottanta contro il gigante Ibm. Golia oggi, contro gli eroi della nuova, nuova frontiera: l'Internet, l'avanguardia libertaria delle autostrade informatiche. E il nuovo Rockefeller, restauratore della supremazia industriale statunitense: il suo software e il linguaggio officiale della Cina che si affaccia alla modernità informatica. Nessun giapponese aveva mai osato volare tanto in alto. Ma è anche il simbolo del nuovo, sottile, potere monopolistico: "Può un privato cittadino diventare proprietario della lingua inglese? Ebbene: Gates vorrebbe possedere l'equivalente informatico dell'inglese" denuncia Michael Spindler, capo della Apple.

Gates, in realtà, rischia molto più di quanto non sembri a prima vista. Nonostante la sua aria da bravo studente, è un giocatore. In novembre, al Comdex, la megafiera dell'informatica di Las Vegas, è stato visto puntare forte al poker, nel casinò del Mirage. Niente però in confronto alla sua vera, interminabile partita, durata tutto il 1995. Nel corso dell'anno Gates si è davvero giocato la leadership nel mercato dei computer.

Già: l'incredibile 1995 del Gates bifronte è una serie di successi tattici accompagnata da una progressiva debolezza strategica, Gates non è solo l'uomo dell'anno per aver comprato ricchi archivi fotografici o un famoso codice leonardesco, per aver lanciato il nuovo programma Windows 95 con la campagna pubblicitaria più spettacolare della storia del software, o per essere entrato in società col mitico regista Steven Spielberg allo scopo di creare divertenti cd-rom, o per aver firmato una joint-venture con la rete tv Nbc destinata a produrre un servizio di informazioni interattivo via cavo 24 su 24. Il suo vero colpo da maestro, la mossa del '95, annuciata giovedi 7 dicembre, è stata la più umile delle decisioni, la più difficile per un eterno vincitore: ammetere di avere sbagliato.

In quell'occasione, implicitamente, Gates ha reso merito alla leggenda della prima parte del '95: la Netscape, lazienda di Marc Andreessen e Jim Clark nata nell'aprile del '94 dall'idea, un po' folle, di distribuire gratis il software per navigare sulla "rete delle reti". La Netscape nell'agosto del '95 si è transformata in una potenza da 2 milliardi di dollari, grazie all'entusiasmo degli investitori di borsa.

La storia della Netscape ha innescato una vera e propria febbre dell'oro informatico. Un'epidemia imprenditoriale e mediatica, partita dalla California, si diffonde a Wall Street e Washington, per poi espandersi sututto il pianeta. L'Internet alimenta i sogni più arditi. L'immaginario collettivo si arricchisce di un nuovo mito: quello del cyberspazio che supera le costrizioni del tempo e della distanza, che garantisce l'accesso di massa all'informazione e all'educazione, che trasforma gli affari e il divertimento. Si realizza la previsione che Nicholas Negroponte, fondatore del Media lab, aveva azzardato nel 1985: la convergenza dei diversi media nell'unico mezzo digitale. Cosi, enormi potenze prendono decisioni reschiose e arrivano le megafusioni di Disney e Abc, Time Warner e Cnn, Ibm e Lotus.

Di fronte a tutto questo, Bill Gates è sembrato per mesi arroccato sulle sue posizioni, tentato di combattere contro tutti per riaffermare il proprio dominio. Potendo schierare un esercito di 150 milioni di computer, almeno l'80 per cento di quelli installati in tutto il mondo, che continua a marciare con il suo software.

In realtà, Gates non ha compreso subito il fenomeno Internet. Anzi, per qualche tempo lo ha snobbato. A chi gli contestava di aver perso un treno, rispondeva senza nascondere un po' di arroganza: "Già, avrò perso almeno una trentina di milioni di dollari". Noccioline . . .

Non se ne stava certo fermo, Gates. Ma la sua idea del futuro dell'informatica era in quel momento fondata molto sul suo passato. Al centro vedeva ancora la logica che aveva costruito is suo potere condiviso con l'Intel di Andrew Grove: un'estenuante rincorsa tra sistemi operativi e software applicativi sempre più complessi destinati a girare su microprocessori sempre più potenti. Una logica cui tutta l'industria dei computer ha dovuto sottostare per un decennio. "Solo un idiota farebbe affari con la Microsoft" si dice nella Silicon Valley "ma anche gli idioti devono mangiare".

Cosi, la stragrande maggioranza dei pc funziona solo montando i sistemi operativi della Microsoft, e dunque paga all'azienda di Gates una "tassa" del valore di circa 1.500 milliardi di lire all'anno. In realtà, sul controllo dei sistemi operativi la Microsoft fonda tra l'altro anche la competitività del suoi programmi applicativi, per esempio quelli che servono a scrivere e far di conto: tanto che, secondo alcune stime, metà del valore del software per pc venduto nel mondo arriva alle casse della Microsoft.

Non stupisce che Gates non desiderasse cambiare questa logica. Il mercato vuole pc sempre più semplici da usare e collegati in rete? La resposta: un nuovo sistema operativo, il Windows 95, più facile e dotato dei comandi chiave per allacciarsi al Microsoft Network (Msn), una rete telematica nata come alternative all'Internet. In un anno, prevedeva Gates, il Windows 95 avrebbe conquistato circa 40 milioni di utenti di pc e molti di questi, con un semplice clic, si sarebbero ritrovati nell'Msn. Il controllo del cuore del pc avrebbe garantito il tato alla riuscita del nuovo network telematico. Un piano quasi perfetto.

word count: 943

Regione Autonoma della Sardegna

LA PRESENTE COPLA COMPOST
DI N°. 4 FOGLI CONFORM.
ALL ORIGINALE EMESSO DA CU-
ESTO UFFICIO.
ASSESSORATO INDUSTRIA
Divisione Miniere

Direttore della Divisione

Le Assessore all'Industria

Dott. Cicero Saba

Visto lo Statuto Speciale per la Sardegna approvato con legge costituzionale 26.2.1948, n. 3 e relative norme di attuazione ;

VISTO il R.D.L. 29.7.1927, N. 1443 e modificazioni ;

VISTA l'istanza 12.1.1981 e la documentazione ad essa allegata, con la quale la CARBOSULCIS S.p.A. - con sede legale in CAGLIARI - Via Dante n° 108 - Cod. Fiscale 00456650928 - chiede la concessione temporanea per la coltivazione di combustibili solidi del giacimento sito in località "Monte Sinni" ricadente in territorio dei comuni di Portoscuso, Gonnesa e Carbonia, provincia di Cagliari ;

CONSIDERATO che l'istanza in sede di pubblicazione nell'Albo Pretorio dei Comuni di Portoscuso, Gonnesa e Carbonia e di inserzione nel Bollettino Ufficiale della Regione Sarda del 20.2.1981 n° 8, parte 3, non ha dato luogo ad opposizioni o reclami ;

VISTO il rapporto dell'Ufficio Distrettuale delle Miniere in data 21.10.1981, n. 3277 ;

VISTO il parere espresso dal Comitato Regionale delle Miniere nella seduta del 22.12.1981 ;

VISTO il verbale di delimitazione in data 28.7.1982 nonchè il piano topografico alla scala 1:25.000 e la monografia dei vertici, citati nel suddetto verbale del quale fanno parte integrante, vistati entrambi dall'Ufficio Distrettuale delle Miniere di Iglesias :

<u>DECRETA</u>

ART. 1 - Alla CARBOSULCIS S.p.A. - con sede legale in CAGLIARI - Via Dante n. 108 - Cod.Fisc. 00456650928 - è concessa la facoltà di coltivare per la durata di anni 30 (trenta) il giacimento minerario di combustibili solidi denominato "Monte Sinni" ricadente in territorio dei comuni di Portoscuso, Gonnesa e Carbonia, Provincia di Cagliari.

ART. 2 - L'area della concessione denominata "Monte Sinni" ha una estensione di Ha 5.940 (cinquemilanovecentoquaranta) e risulta delimitata in rosso sul piano topografico alla scala 1:25.000 e descritta nel verbale di delimitazione, citato in premessa, piano e verbale che si allegano al presente decreto perchè ne facciano parte integrante come Allegato A) e Allegato B).

ART. 3 - La Società Concessionaria è tenuta a far pervenire all'Assessorato Industria - Divisione Miniere - entro due mesi dalla data di consegna, copia autentica della nota di avvenuta trascrizione del presente decreto presso la Conservatori dei Registri Immobiliari competente per territorio ;

ART. 4 - A norma e per gli effetti del paragrafo 1) art. 40 del R.D.L. 29.7.1927, n.1443 il concessionario è tenuto :

1) - a trasmettere mensilmente all'Assessorato Industria-Divisione Miniere - e all'Ufficio Distrettuale delle Miniere, entro il giorno otto di ciascun mese, l'apposito prospetto debitamente compilato con i dati statistici in esso specificati e con la relazione sull'andamento dei lavori e dei risultati ottenuti ;

2) - a trasmettere i risultati dei lavori geofisici eventualmente eseguiti ;

3) - a conservare i campioni geologici, attraversati nelle ricerche ;

4) - ad effettuare la denuncia di esercizio al Distretto Minerario di Iglesias, almeno otto giorni prima dell'inizio o della ripresa dei lavori, con lettera raccomandata con avviso di ricevimento ai sensi degli artt. 24-25-26 e 27 del D.P.R. 9.4.1959, n. 128

5) - a fornire ai funzionari della Divisione Miniere dell'Assessorato Industria e dell'Ufficio Distrettuale delle Miniere di Iglesias tutti i mezzi necessari per visitare i lavori ed a comunicare, i dati che venissero comunque richiesti.

ART. 5 - Ai sensi della L.R. 9.10.1959, n. 17 "è fatto obbligo alla Ditta (appaltatrice, concessionaria, mutuataria, autorizzata) a praticare e far praticare a favore dei lavoratori dipendenti o sub dipendenti, condizioni di lavoro non inferiori a quelli risultanti dai contratti collettivi di categoria vigenti nella provincia, e, in assenza di tali contratti collettivi stipulate in sede provinciale, di applicare e fare applicare i contratti collettivi nazionali di categoria.

- le infrazioni a tale obbligo e alle leggi sul lavoro accertate dall'Ispettorato del Lavoro ai sensi del D.P.R. 13.9.1955, n.520, e notificate all'Amministrazione Regionale, danno luogo a diffida con termine di giorni cinque e quindi all'adozione delle sequenti misure :

a) - per ritardato pagamento dei salari o per corresponsione dei medesimi in misura inferiore a quella contrattuale, indennità di mora del 10% del debito da corrispondersi ai lavoratori interessati, elevabile al 25 % in caso di recidiva ;

b) - per mancata osservanza delle norme relative ad istituti contrattuali diversi dal salario o dalle percezioni in denaro, diffida formale da parte degli Organi di Vigilanza ;

c) - in caso di perdurante inadempienza constatata dagli Organi di Vigilanza, decadenza del rapporto oggetto del presente atto, secondo le procedure pre-
Dei rilievi a carico della Società per mancata osservanza dei contratti collettivi del lavoro e delle leggi sul lavoro, sarà tenuta opportune annotazione agli atti dell'Amministrazione Regionale. Restano salve le disposizioni della L.R. 6.3.1956, n. 8.

ART. 6 - La Ditta concessionaria è inoltre tenuta :

a) - a presentare entro l'ultimo trimestre di ciascun anno ed ad attuare nel corso dell'anno successivo il programma dei lavori di coltivazione e di ricerca approvato dall'Autorità Mineraria Regionale ;

b) - a corrispondere alla Regione il diritto annuo anticipato di £. 3.200 per ogni ettaro o frazione di superficie compresa nell'area della concessione e complessivamenta di £. 19.008.000. =

c) - a corrispondere il diritto fisso di £. 331.000 a termine del D. L. n.787 del 27.12.1981.

ART. 7 - La concessione è accordata senza pregiudizio degli eventuali diritti dei terzi.

ART. 8 - Il presente decreto sarà trasmesso alla Corte dei Conti per la registrazione, pubblicato nel Bollettino Ufficiale della Regione Sarda e trascritto presso la Conservatoria dei RR.II. competente per territorio.=

Cagliari, addì

[ ]CORTE DEI CONTI
REGIONE SARDA
Data 24.11.1982 L'ASSESSORE
Registro n. 1 [ ]n. 19 - COSSU - [signature]
([ ])

word count: 928

Di seguito verranno brevemente esposti i caratteri che contraddistinguono i litotipi della seguenze deposizionale analizzata.

1. 1. **Litotipi "sterili"**

Calcari

Tale litotipo è presente in tutti i livelli della successione studiata ed è caratterizzato dal colore, grigio nella parte basale (miliolitico) e beige-nocciola nel "Produttivo", dal contenuto di materiale organico talvolta disposto in livelletti di spessore anche centimetrico e dal contenuto in resti fossili.

A tal proposito infatti nei calcari beige-nocciola si possono osservare molto spesso banchi di calcare ricchi in frammenti di gusci di lamellibranchi e gasteropodi di dimensioni variabilissiem (lumachelle) oppure livelli altrettanto ricchi in oogoni di Characee (organi di riproduzione di alghe verdi) o gusci di ostracodi; nei calcari grigi invece sono generalmente prevalenti le faune a miliolidi; più spesso sia i calcari grigi che quelli beigenocciola contengono abbondanti tracce di radici carbonificate e meno frequentemente piritizzate o parzialmente piritizzate.

Dal punto di vista geometrico i calcari beige si presentano in strati di spessore variabile tra i 3 cm e i 100-150 cm con pseudolaminazioni piano parallele, oppure in lenti convesse. Apparentemente la convessità di tali lenti sembrerebbe legata a fenomèni di boudinage tettonico, spesso riscontrabili anche lungo le gallerie della miniera.

Frequentemente i calcari sono interessati da intensa fratturazione dovuta sia a compressioni (piccole falie inverse con piani inclinati 30°- 45°, riconoscibili a scala del campione), sia a movimenti distensivi (faglie di più grandi dimensioni che spesso causano ricristallizzazione di calcite lungo i piani di rottura) che talvolta provocano uncinature negli strati.

Marne ed Argilliti

Questi litotipi sempre presenti nella sequenza descritta sono caratterizzati dalla variabilità del loro colore (rossastro nella parte alta, grigio scuro o grigio-olivastro rispettivamente verso il centro ed alla base della serie), dalla facilità con cui, in certi casi, si disgregano in acqua, dalla presenza di frammenti di gusci e modelli interni di gasteropodi parzialmente o totalmente piritizzati, dalla presenza di concrezioni e septarie di dimensioni variabili e dall'alto contenuto in materiale organico (piante anche ben conservate) e pirite (cristallini diffusi).

Lo spessore di questi due litotipi è variabilissimo e va da un minimo di 5 cm ad un massimo di 200 cm.

In genere sia le argilliti che la marne possono presentare una debole laminazione parallela al bedding, ma più spesso sono omogenee o riemogeneizzate da radici o bioturbazioni animali.

Frequentemente gli intervalli argillosi e marnosi si presentano brecciati e/o minutamente fratturati e scagliettati, soprattutto in vicinanza di disturbi tettonici soprastanti o sottostanti.

Microconglomerati, Arenarie, Siltiti

Queste tre litologie sono comuni in tutti i sondaggi descritti e sono caratterizzati non tanto dal loro colore, che varia tra il grigio chiaro ed il grigio scuro, quanto dal loro spessore, dalla loro continuità laterale, dalla presenza di particolari strutture sedimentarie, dal contenuto fossilifero, dal contenuto in materiale organico e dalla monogenicità o poligenicità del clasti costituenti i litotipi stessi.

Cosi, per esempio, nei microconglomerati o nelle arenarie si possono frequentemente ritrovare intervalli clastici a base erosiva, con caratteristiche sequenze a granulometria crescente o decrescente, passaggi litologici sfumati o netti, con strutture tipo stratificazione e laminazione incrociata a basso angolo o piano parallela mentre nelle arenarie fini e nelle siltiti è più probabile rinvenire strutture di deformazione da carico o tipo flaser, livelli con abbondanti resti di gusci di molluschi, bioturbati o con concrezioni anche di grosse dimensioni.

I clasti che costituiscono questi litotipi sono essenzialmente quarzosi o formati da calcite, ben cerniti, mal classati subarrotondati, ma in qualche caso sono stati osservati elementi argillosi o di carbone di grosse dimensioni (fino a 6-7 cm di diametro) arrotondati e deformati, di chiara origine intraformazionale.

Dal punto di vista geometrico i corpi clastici formati da questi litotipi si presentano eteropici con tutte le altre litologie e mostrano caratteristiche chiusure laterali lentiformi.

Il loro spessore è variabilissimo e comunque mediamente compreso tra il metro e i 10-12 mctri.

1.2. Carbone, carbone impuro, argilla nera carboniosa e scisto carbonioso

Sulla base del contenuto argilloso, sono stati distinti quattro tipi di rocce carboniose:

scisto carbonioso	contenuto argilloso > 90 %	carbonaceous shale
argilla nera carboniosa	contenuto argilloso 50÷90%	coaly shale
carbone impuro	contenuto argilloso 10÷50%	impure coal
carbone	contenuto argilloso < 10%	coal

La determinazione macroscopica della quantità di materiale argilloso è un'operazione molto soggettiva ma non tale da portare a confondere i litotipi con percentuale di impurità molto diverse.

In qualche caso i problemi di distinzione sono legati all'effetto della tettonica, responsabile della creazione di strutture plicative (drag folds) a piccola scala o, per tratti a volte decimetrici, di fitti piani di taglio testimoniati da slickensides.

Questi quattro litotipi si ritrovano generalmente associati a formare il seam, di cui costituiscono la parte minerariamente interessante, alternati l'uno l'altro o intercalate con livelli generalmente calcareo-marnosi.

La continuità e lo spessore di quasi tutti i seams sono state accertate, come vedremo in seguito, con il lavoro di correlazione litostratigrafica dei sondaggi esaminati.

word count: 808

Calcolo degli investimenti previsti dalla Regione Sarda

Abbiamo calcolato gli investimenti previsti per realizzare la soluzione proposta dalla Regione Sarda e quelle che seguono sono le considerazioni che giustificano i valori esposti:

centrale Sulcis terzo gruppo esistente: questo gruppo, il pi nuovo dei tre, sar destinato a marciare con un mix di carbone di importazione e carbone Sulcis nulla fase di avviamento della miniera per poi essere sottoposto a revamping. Per questa centrale abbiamo accettato quanto ha previsto I'ENEL per inserire impianti di DeSox e DeNox che tutavia, poich sono stati dimensionati per carbone di importazione, richiedono un investimento proporzionalmente inferiore in funzione del bassissimo contenuto di zolfo;

nuova centrale IGCC: sebbene le nostre valutazioni con elementi di costo provenienti dal mercato internazionale della componentistica termoelettrica e chimica ci abbiano portato a costi di investimento sensibilmente inferiori, ad evitare inutili polemiche o contestazioni, che in questa fase consideriamo improduttive, abbiamo deciso di fare riferimento al costo previsto per la prima centrale europea a carbone pulito che la Elcogas realizzer a Puertollano in Spagna. Ovviamente poich gli in siti perfettamente attrezzati perch sede di esistenti centrali termoelettriche e quindi dotati delle infrastrutture e di tutti i servizi communi e generali, ragionevole prevedere una riduzione di costo. Ed ancora, poich proponiamo un investimento realizzato da una Societ elettrica, e non da un consorzio internazionale che beneficia di una serie di contribute che comprensibile giustificare con budgets prudenti, possibile prevedere una ulteriore riduzione di costo. In definitive riteniamo corretto e prudenziale per un impianto IGCC della potenza di questo progetto indicare un costo specifico di 2,32 Milioni di lire per KW installato.

centrale Sulcis revamping: il revamping consiste in un intervento di manutenzione straordinaria dei due primi gruppi della centrale Sulcis, l'inserimento del ciclo combinato di tipo topping con alimentazione a gas di sintesi prodotto mediante gassificazione del carbone.

centrale Portoscuso revamping: l'intervento dello tipo adottato per la centrale Sulcis, viene programmato in tempi successive perch la centrale in migliori condizioni ed essenziale per I'alimentazione dell'adiacente elettrolisi dell'alluminio (240 MW continui). Vi da segnalare che l'intervento si presenta di caratteristiche tecniche molto interessanti per via del particolare disegno della centrale che rende favorevole la cogenerazione.

Quanto sopra esposto è chiaramente mostrato nella tabella seguente:

2 Schema proposto dalla Regione Sarda

Tabella degli investimenti		esistente RAS	soluzione ENEL	soluzione
Centrale Sulcis 3e esistente	GLit			419
Centrale Sulcis Nuova	GLit			2.288
Nuova centrale IGCC	GLit		780	
Centrale Sulcis 1 revamping	GLit		496	
Centrale Sulcis 2 revamping	GLit		496	
Totale 1^{e} fase	GLit		1.279	2.707
margins consume Sulcis	GLit		492	
Centrale Portoscuso revamping	GLit		1.006	
Centrale Sulcis 3 revamping	GLit		496	
Totale investimenti	GLit		3.273	2.707
Investimenti previsti da ENEL	GLit		3.415	-708

la configurazione proposta dalla Regione consente di smaltire tutta la produzione mineraria attualmente prevista, ne consente importanti sviluppi, nel totale rispetto della legislazione in materia ambientale vigente e futura (ben pi restrittiva);

L'investimento specifico per KW netto installato del 40% inferiore rispetto a quello richiesto dagli impianti programmati da ENEL, prendendo a base i costi esposti da ENEL;

3 Schema proposto dalla Regione Sarda				
Tabella degli investimenti specifici		esistente	soluzione RAS	soluzione ENEL
Centrale Sulcis 3^{e} esistente	KLit/KW			1.922
Centrale Sulcis Nuova	KLit/KW			5.248
Nuova centrale IGCC	KLit/KW		2.320	
Centrale Sulcis 1 revamping	KLit/KW		1.740	
Centrale Sulcis 2 revamping	KLit/KW		1.740	
CentraIe Portoscuso revamping	KLit/KW		1.796	
Centrale Sulcis 3 revamping	KLit/KW		1.740	
Totale investimenti specifici	KLit/KW		1.803	4.139
Differenza investimenti specifici		KLit/KW		-2.336

l'energia prodotta dalla configurazione proposta dalla Regione Sardegna pari a pi del doppio di quella prodotta con la configurazione ENEL. A questo proposito vi da precisare che l'impianto IGCC viene considerato in quanto generatore di energia elettrica di disponibilit pari ad un impianto convenzionale. Ci perch esso sar naturalmente dotato della possibilit di utilizzare anche un combustibile liquido nella eventualit che nel primo anno di esercizio la parte chimica presenti problemi di giovinezza. Pertanto viene assegnato a questo impianto un coefficiente di utilizzazione della potenza di 7.500 ore/anno, cos come previsto nell'impianto SARAS di Sarroch, la cui parte a gassificazione pu considerarsi di tipo tradizionale e conosciuta giacch tratta TAR di raffineria.

4 Schema proposto dalla Regione Sarda				
Tabella dell'energia prodotta		esistente	soluzione	soluzione
		RAS	ENEL	
Centrale Sulcis 3^{e} esistente	GWh/anno	3.375		1.090
Centrale Sulcis Nuova	GWh/anno			2.616
Nuova centrale IGCC	GWh/anno		2.016	
Centrale Sulcis 1 revamping	GWh/anno		1.710	
Centrale Sulcis 2 revamping	GWh/anno		1.710	
Totale 1^{e} fase	GWh/anno		*4.267*	*3.706*
margine consumo Sulcis	Gwh/anno		1.169	
CentraIe Portoscuso revamping	GWh/anno		3.360	
Centrale Sulcis 3 revamping	GWh/anno	340	1.710	0
Totale potenze fase finale	GWh/anno	3.715	10.506	3.706
Differenza potenze	GWh/anno		**-6.791**	**- 6.800**

i consumi specifici per un impianto IGCC funzionante con carbone Sulcis sono di 1911 Kcal/KWh, mentre con carbone di importazione questo conusmo scende a 1890 Kcal/KWh;

le discariche per le ceneri prodotte dagli impianti IGCC sono tecnicamente poco impegnative e di classe inferiore (Tipo 2A) in quanto trattasi di materiali non inquinanti perch chimicamente e fisicamente inerti;

la tecnologia IGCC consente di valorizzare con il revamping la centrale Portoscuso, conservando il capitale di una centrale recente e l'occupazione di personale, ed ottenendo nuova potenza a costi inferiori rispetto a quelli da sostenere per un impianto nuovo

in definitiva questa tecnologia consente di sviluppare veramente negli anni a venire l'industria cel carbone de Sulcis ottenendo il risultato di produrre energia elettrica con alti rendimenti, nel rispetto dell'ambiente, sfruttando gli impianti esistenti ed utilizzando una ricchezza locale di dimensioni imponenti.

word count: 932

ASSIGNMENT 1 - TRANSLATION

Bill opens the Gates of Internet

"Bill Gates is the most enthusiastic businessman of the century," snaps Jack Weldon, head of General Electric. "Microsoft is the greatest economic power in the United States," maintains Eric Schmidt, manager of Sun Microsystems. "Microsoft will be a priority political problem for the next 20 years, " predicts Mitchell Kapor, founder of Lotus.

William Henry Gates III. Bill. The two-faced Janus of American industry. The bridge between the past of the PCs and the future of the information society. The David of the Eighties versus giant IBM; today's Goliath against the heroes of the new "new frontier:" the Internet, libertarian vanguard of the information highways. He is the new Rockefeller, the restorer of the United States' industrial supremacy: his software is the official language of China as it moves out into the modem world of data processing. No Japanese ever dared fly that high. But he is also the symbol of new, subtle monopolistic power: "Can a private citizen become the owner of the English language? Well, Gates could own the data processing equivalent of English," charges Michael Spindler, head of Apple.

In reality, Gates is risking much more than might appear at first sight. In spite of his "good-boy" air, he is a gambler. He was seen in November at Comdex, the Las Vegas data processing megafair, betting heavily on poker at the Mirage casino. But that was nothing compared to his real, endless game throughout all of 1995. That year, Gates actually gambled away his leadership in the computer market.

So two-faced Gates' incredible 1995 turned out to be a series of tactical successes, paralleled by a progressive strategic weakness. Gates is the man of the year not only for having bought a rich photographic archive or a famous Leonardesque codex; for having launched the new Windows 95 program with the most spectacular advertising drive in the history of software; or for having teamed up with the mythic director Steven Spielberg for the purpose of creating CD-ROM entertainment; or for having signed a joint-venture contract with NBC-TV to produce an interactive, round-the-clock cable news service. His real masterstroke - the master-move of '95, announced on Thursday, December 7 - was the humblest decision, the most difficult for an eternal winner: to admit having been wrong.

On that occasion, Gates implicitly credited the legend of the first half of '95: Netscape, the outfit of Marc Andreessen and Jim Clark, born in April '94 from the slightly nutty idea of distributing - gratis - software for navigating the "supernetwork. " In August '95, Netscape became a $2 billion power thanks to the enthusiasm of stock market investors.

The story of Netscape triggered a real data processing gold fever. A business and media epidemic started from

California and spread to Wall Street and Washington, thence to fan out all over the planet. The Internet feeds the most ardent dreams. A new myth enriches the collective imagination: that of a cyberspace that overcomes the constraints of time and distance, that guarantees mass access to information and education, that transforms business and entertainment. The prediction that Media lab founder Nicholas Negroponte ventured in 1985 is now coming true: the convergence of the diverse media in a single digital tool. In this way, enormous powers make risky decisions and come up with the megamergers of Disney and ABC, Time-Warner and CNN, IBM and Lotus.

Against this background, Bill Gates seemed ensconced in his positions for months, tempted to fight everybody to reassert his rule. He was able to marshal an army of 150 million computers - at least 80 percent of those installed all over the world - that continues to operate with his software.

In reality, Gates did not immediately grasp the Internet phenomenon. For some time, he even snubbed it. And if somebody told him that he had missed the boat, he would reply, without in the least hiding his arrogance: "So I lost at least $30 million. " Peanuts . . .

Gates certainly did not mark time. But at that moment, his idea of the future of data processing was based very much on his past. In essence, he was still focusing on the logic that built the power which he shared with Andrew Grove's Intel: a wearisome runoff between ever more complex operating systems and applications software, destined to revolve around ever more powerful microprocessors. A logic to which the computer industry had to submit for a decade. "Only an idiot would do business with Microsoft" - so they say in Silicon valley - "but even an idiot must eat."

And so, the overwhelming majority of PCs are working only with Microsoft operating systems, and therefore pay Gates' outfit a value-added "tax" of around 1,500 billion lire per year. In reality, Microsoft uses control over operating systems, among other things, to underpin the competitiveness of its applications programs - for example, those that are employed to write and do the accounts - so much so, that according to some estimates, half of the PC software value sold worldwide winds up in Microsoft's coffers.

It is not surprising that Gates would not want to change that logic. Does that market want PCs that are ever simpler to use and that are networked? The answer: a new operating system, Windows 95, easier and equipped with key controls to link up with the Microsoft Network (MSN) - a data transmission network created as an alternative to the Internet. Within a year, predicts Gates, Windows 95 will have won about 40 million PC users, and many of them could wind up in the MSN with a simple click. Control over the very core of the PC business will by then have ensured the new system's success, and that in turn will have led to the successful outcome of the new data transmission network. An almost perfect plan.

... *del secolo* " (line 5) - There is no comma in the Italian text after *secolo.* Be sure to put a comma in the English text.

Giano bifronte (line 10) - Two-faced Janus. This is somewhat of a redundancy in the original, since the god Janus implies a two-faced creature. Moreover, in English the expression "two-faced" is derogatory, while in the mythological original it does not quite have the same connotation. Perhaps "Janus" should be left in translation without "two-faced," or else expound to: "Janus (the god with two faces) of American industry." This is a tough call.

pc (line 10) - In English PC is always capitalized. If one is used to reading about computers in Italian and seeing this term in lowercase, it is easy to make the mistake of rendering it in English in lowercase as well. Remember the rule of the "two persons," and when you translate into English, think English.

Ibm (line 11) - Always IBM in English.

modernità informatica (line 14) - Translated "data processing," *informatica* could also be translated "informatics," or "computer science." These terms overlap, and "data processing" seems to fit into this context of a non-scientific, popular article.

bravo studente (line 19-20) - Translated as "good boy;" one could probably come up with a "zippier" term.

In novembre (line 20) - Here is a good example of a sentence that needs to be "rearranged" in the target language in order to make sense of the source language text. There is no one way of rearranging this sentence, but rather it comes down to a common sense decision of how to arrange the words so that the translation is clear and makes good sense.

Leadership, computer (line 22) - You attention is drawn to the "invasion" by English of another language, in this case Italian. Here "leadership" and "computer" means exactly what they mean in the original language, but this is not always the case. Beware of borrowed English words in other languages. Oftentimes, the meaning is altered by the time the word is given a new home in the host language.

accompagnata (line 24) - This could be translated as "accompanied by." The translator chose "along with," which is purely preferential.

... *leonardesco,* (line 26) - Here a semicolon works better for this complex sentence than a comma. See note about punctuation in Section 1.

implicitamente, (line 33) - Here the word "implicitly" was put after the subject, rather than before. The proper placing of words in a sentence is one of the most important functions of good writing, and, for that matter, good translation. It makes all the difference between a lucid, easy-to-read text, and an awkward, hard-to-read one.

vera e propria febbre dell'oro informatico (line page 2, line 2) - This phrase is somewhat hard to translate. *Vera e propna* can be rendered simply as "real." The rest of the sentence could be possible rendered as "information gold fever."

marciare (line 13) - Literally "march," or "go with," in this context the proper word is it operate," or "work. " The danger of mistranslating cognate words and terms in closely related languages like English and Italian is real and apparent, and must be guarded against.

1.500 milliardi di lire (lines 27) - here the period in numbers of 1000 changes to a comma in English, a minor point with major implications.

Autonomous Region of Sardinia

THIS COPY CONSISTS
OF No. 4 SHEETS AND IS
EQUIVALENT TO THE
ORIGINAL ISSUED BY
THIS OFFICE
COMMISSION OF INDUSTRY
Division of Mines
Division Director

Commissioner of Industry

Dr. Omero Saba

WHEREAS the Special Articles for Sardinia approved by Constitutional Law No. 3 of 2/26/1948 and related norms of implementation [and]

WHEREAS Royal Decree Law (RDL) No. 1443 of 7/29/1927 and its revisions, [and]

WHEREAS the petition of 1/12/1981 and its attached documentation ,by which CARBOSULCIS S.p.A. -
with its registered office in CAGLIARI, Via Dante 108, Tax Number 00456650928 - requests a temporary permit for the exploitation of solid fuel in the deposit located in the area of "Monte Sinni" situated in the territory of the towns of Portoscuso, Gonnesa, and Carbonia, Province of Cagliari; [and]

HAVING CONSIDERED that upon publication of the petition in the Magistrate's Register for the Towns
of Portoscuso, Gonnesa, and Carbonia, and its insertion in the Official Bulletin of the Region of Sardinia of 2/20/1981, No. 8, Part 3, it did not elicit any challenges or claims; [and]

WHEREAS the report by the District Office of Mines No. 3277 dated 10/21/1981; [and]

WHEREAS the opinion expressed by the Regional Committee on Mines at its meeting of 12/22/1981; [and]

WHEREAS the statement on boundaries dated 7/28/1982 as well as the topographical plan scaled at 1:25,000 and the monograph on the summits, cited in the aforementioned statement of which they constitute an integral part, both approved by the Iglesias District Office of Mines:

[THEREFORE I HEREBY] **DECREE**

ARTICLE 1 - Permission to exploit the solid fuel mineral deposit named "Monte Sinni, " situated in the

territory of the towns of Portoscuso, Gonnesa, and Carbonia, Province of Cagliari, is given to CARBOSULCIS S.p.A., with registered office in CAGLIARI, Via Dante 108, Tax Number 00456650928, for the term of 30 (thirty) years.

ARTICLE 2 - The area of the concession named "Monte Sinni" covers 5,940 (five thousand nine hundred

forty) hectares and is outlined in red on the topographical plan at a scale of 1:25,000 and described in the statement on boundaries, cited in the premise, said plan and record being attached to this decree so that they constitute an integral part of it as Appendix A) and Appendix B).

ARTICLE 3 - The Concessionaire Company is required to send, within two months of its delivery, to the

Office of the Assessor of Industry, Division of Mines, an authentic copy of the memorandum of the completed recording of this decree at the Registrar's Office having jurisdiction over that area;

ARTICLE 4 - According to the regulations and for the purposes of Paragraph 1, Art. 40, RDL [Royal Decree Law] No. 1443 of 7/29/1927, the concessionaire is required:

1) - to send to the Office of the Assessor of Industry, Division of Mines, and to the District Office of Mines, every month and by the eighth day of the month, the appropriate summary, duly compiled, with the statistical data specified in it and with a report on the progress of operations and obtained results;

1) - to send the results of geophysical work that might be undertaken;

3) - to preserve geological samples encountered during exploration;

4) - to make a declaration of work to the Iglesias Mining District, at least eight days before the

initiation of resumption of operations, by means of a registered letter with a delivery receipt in accordance with Arts. 24, 25, 26, and 27 of the Decree of the President of the Republic (DPR) No. 128 of 4/9/1959;

5) - to supply the officials of the Division of Mines of the Office of the Assessor of Industry and the Iglesias District Office of Mines with all those means necessary for visiting the operations and, in any event, to forward requested information.

ARTICLE 5 - In accordance with Regional Law (LR) No. 17 of 10/9/1959,

"the Company (contractor, concessionaire, borrower, authorized) is obliged to practice and have practiced, on behalf of its own and subcontractor employees, work conditions that are not inferior to those resulting from collective agreements in effect for the same business category in the province, and, in absence of such collective agreements stipulated at the provincial level, to apply and have applied the national collective agreements for this category.

- Infractions of this requirement and of labor laws that are verified by the Labor Inspectorate in accordance with DPR No. 520 of 9/13/1955, and reported to the Regional Administration, lead to a warning with a deadline of five days and then to the adoption of the following measures:

a) - for late payment of wages and for wage payments that are lower than the contracted rate, a late fee of 10% of the debt to be paid to workers involved, which can be raised to 25% in case of recidivism;

b) - for failure to observe the regulations concerning those contractual provisions other than wages and monetary receipts, a formal warning by the enforcement agencies;

c) - in the event of persistent non-compliance confirmed by the enforcement agencies, lapse of the relationship that is the object of this document, according to the procedures pre-[sic] For statements against the Company for failure to observe the collective labor agreements and labor laws, an appropriate entry will be made in the records of the Regional Administration. The dispositions in LR No. 8 of 3/6/1956 are excepted.

Likewise excepted are the orders that the Labor Inspectorate might adopt within the limits of its institutional jurisdiction.

ARTICLE 6 - The concessionaire Company is further required:

a) - to present its program for mining and exploration operations approved by the Regional Mining Authority by the last quarter of each year and to carry it out in the following year;

b) - to pay the Region the annual advance fee of £ 3,200 for each hectare or fraction of surface comprised in the area of the concession, for a total of £ 19,008,000.

c) - to pay the fixed fee of £331,000 in accordance with Decree Law No.787 of 12/27/1981.

ARTICLE 7 - The concession is made without prejudice to the possible rights of third parties.

ARTICLE 8 - This decree shall be forwarded to the Court of Audit for registration, published in the Official Bulletin of the Region of Sardinia, and recorded at the Recorder's Office with jurisdiction for the area.

Cagliari, on

[illegible] COURT OF AUDIT
REGION OF SARDINIA

date 11/24/1982 THE COMMISSIONER
Register No. 1 [illegible] No. 19 - COSSU - [signature]
[illegible]
([signed illegible])

ASSIGNMENT 2 - NOTES

General comments:

a. Subject matter

This text represents a specific area of law, namely, business law as it applies to a legal permit. With this in mind, one should be sensitive to the fact that this original Italian text, which relates to granting concession to a company on the island of Sardinia, reflects Italian law as practiced in the Autonomous Region of Sardinia, and therefore the language does not exactly coincide with either British or U.S. legal usage. The present translation attempts to put the text in understandable American legal language, albeit this presents certain difficulties. The general intent is to make the translation clear and unequivocal. The original document ought to remain the legally binding version.

b. Format

We draw your attention to the fact that the original text is typed in a legal Italian format, following established rules. Therefore, the English translation was formatted to look like the original, and each page of translation corresponds to each page of the original. This was done for several good reasons: (a) an end-user of a translation would often need to compare the two texts, and this exact replication makes it very easy to compare, and also to make sure nothing is missing; (b) it helps the translator to check hislher own work, making sure nothing was left out; and (c) it conveys the sense of orderliness which is critical in legal documents.

Visto (line 18) - "Whereas" is the official translation, but in American legal documents it is usually followed by a full sentence with a verb, which is not the case here. It may be better to do some editing on this text, but this creates the risk of altering the meaning. A translator's note on a separate sheet of paper may be in order, so as to explain the problems of translating this text.

R.D.L. (line 18) - This may require some research as to the expansion of this abbreviation. An Italian legal dictionary may be useful in this instance.

DECRETA (page 2, line 13) - Here the English translation adds in brackets [THEREFORE I HEREBY], to make the original text conform with American legal usage. The brackets indicate that the enclosed text does not appear in the original, and is only used for elucidation. In American legal documents, "whereas" is always followed by "therefore."

5.940 (line 24) - The period in Italian in numbers over 1000 becomes a comma in English.

- Divisione Minieri - (line 33) - The separation by dashes of a sub-item changes in English to a comma.

29.7.1927 (line 40) - Italian dates start with the day, followed by the month and year, whereas American English usage starts with the month, followed by the day and year.

[ ] (page 5, lines 16, 17, 21) - This blank space represents illegible text, which is rendered in the translation as [illegible]. This often happens with legal documents, where there are notations or signatures which cannot be deciphered. Unless absolutely sure, do not translate such text or try to venture any guesses.

Additional observations:

Since legal documents such as business permits and agreements contain a fairly standard text, you may want to get hold of one or more texts of such English-language documents, to familiarize yourself with their style and terminology. Clearly, one does not always have the time and means to obtain this kind of information, but if this is a subject you expect to translate fairly regularly, it is worth the effort.

Also, it is important to know the purpose of a particular translation, although a translator is not always given this information by the client. If it is to be used as a legally binding document, it has to be accurate to the point of being accepted as such. On the other hand, if it is only for information purposes —say the end-user in this case does not read Italian —then you need not spend nearly as much time and effort to make sure every single word is the best possible equivalent of the original.

The distinguishing features of the lithotypes from the analyzed depositional sequence will be briefly described as follows.

1. 1. Lithotypes of tailings

Limestones

This lithotype is present at all levels of the studied sequence and is characterized by its color, gray in the basal portion (miliolithic) and beige-light brown in the ore-bearing portion, by its organic material content, occasionally disposed in bands that can even be only a few centimeters thick, and by its fossil content.

Indeed, in regard to the beige-light brown limestones, it is very often possible to observe limestone beds containing an abundance of bivalve and gastropod shells in a wide range of sizes (shell-rich limestones) or similarly abundant quantities of Characeae oogonia (reproductive organs of green algae), or Ostracoda shells; in the gray limestones, Miliolidae fauna generally prevail instead; more often, both the gray and beige-light brown limestones contain abundant traces of roots transformed into coal and, less frequently, wholly or partially transformed into pyrite.

From the geometric standpoint, the beige limestones occur in strata whose thickness varies from 3 cm to 100-150 cm with parallel planar pseudo-bands, or in convex lenses. Apparently, the convexity of these lenses would seem to be linked to phenomena of tectonic boudinage, often observable even in mine tunnels.

Frequently, the limestones exhibit intense fracturing, stemming both from compression (small inverse faults with inclined planes of 30° - 45°, observable in the sampling), and from spreading movements (larger faults that often cause recrystallization of calcite along the rupture planes), which occasionally cause hooking in the strata.

Marls and Shales

Always present in the described sequence, these lithotypes are characterized by the variety of their colors (reddish in the upper part, dark gray or olive-gray respectively towards the center and lower part of the series), by the facility with which they disintegrate in water, by the presence of shell fragments and internal models of gastropods that have been partially or totally transformed into pyrite, by the presence of ballstones and septarian nodules of varying sizes, and by their high content of organic material (even well-preserved plants) and pyrite (diffused crystals).

The thickness of these two lithotypes is highly varied, going from a minimum of 5 cm to a maximum of 200 cm.

In general, both the shales and the marls display weak banding parallel to the bedding, but more often they are homogeneous or rehomogenized by roots or animal disturbances.

Frequently, the shale and marl intervals are pulverized and/or minutely fractured and crushed, especially in the neighborhood of overlying or underlying tectonic disturbances.

Microconglomerates, Sandstones, Siltstones

These three lithologies are common in all the described test hole samples and are not characterized so much by their color, which varies between light and dark gray, as by their thickness, lateral continuity, presence of particular sedimentary structures, fossil content, organic material content, and the monogenic or polygenic clasts constituting the lithotypes themselves.

Therefore, in the microconglomerates or sandstones, for example, it is frequently possible to find clastic intervals of an erosive nature, with characteristic sequences of increasing or decreasing granulometry, blurred or distinct lithological passages, with such structural types as stratification and banding crossed at a small angle or on a parallel plane, while in the fine sandstones and siltstones, it is more probable to find burden or flaser type deformation structures, and bands with abundant remains of mollusk shells, and disturbed by animal movements or with ballstones that can reach large dimensions.

The clasts which constitute these lithotypes are essentially quartzitic or formed from calcite, and well sorted, badly classified pebbles, but in some cases large (up to 6-7 cm in diameter), rounded or deformed argillaceous or coal elements, of clearly intraformational origin, have been observed.

From the geometric standpoint, the clastic bodies formed by these lithotypes are heterotopous in comparison with all the other lithologies and present characteristic, lensshaped lateral closures.

Their thickness is highly varied and ranges on average between 1 and 10-12 meters.

1.2. Coal, impure coal, carbonaceous black clay, and carbonaceous schist

Four types of carbonaceous rock have been distinguished on the basis of their argillaceous content:

carbonaceous schist carbonaceous black clay impure coal	coal	argillaceous content > 90 % argillaceous content 50-90%

argillaceous content 10-50%	carbonaceous shale
argillaceous content < 1 0 %	coaly shale
	impure coal
	coal

The macroscopic determination of the quantity of argillaceous material is a highly subjective process, but not so much as to cause confusion with lithotypes of very different percentages of impurity.

In some cases, the problem of making distinctions is connected to tectonic effects, responsible for the formation of drag folds on a small scale or, in sections that can be dozens of centimeters thick, of thick shear planes attested to by slickensides.

These four lithotypes are generally found together in the formation of a seam, comprising the part which is of interest for mining, and alternating with each other or interlayered with levels that are generally calcareous and marly.

The continuity and thickness of almost all the seams have been ascertained, as we shall see below, by the litho-stratigraphic correlations of the examined test hole samples.

ASSIGNMENT 3 - NOTES

General comments:

a. Subject matter

When translating a scientific text, bear in mind that very often several disciplines may come into play in the same material. In this case, the general subject matter is coal mining. This is a broad area that may require the translator to have an understanding of such disciplines as geology, chemistry (both organic and inorganic), mine engineering, meteorology, and many more. Unlike a researcher in a given discipline, or a student of a given subject, the translator is called upon to render all the different aspects of a given subject matter into another language. This does not make the translator an expert in every scientific subject, but it does require a general understanding of a great many disciplines.

b. References

This text is full of scientific terms, which should not deter the translator, since good scientific dictionaries, both Italian-English and English alone, should have, if not all of these terms, at least the vast majority. There is always a chance of running into a term that does not appear in the dictionary, in which case consulting experts is the next best thing to do.

c. Style

While technical and scientific texts appear to be very straightforward, with little need to pay special attention to the writing style, the truth is that it is very easy to become caught up in the need to translate the scientific data and the terminology accurately and completely, while the basic elements of style are being neglected, and as a result the text becomes confused and hard to read. Good writing is the domain not only of literature and the humanities, but also of scientific writing. In translating a text such as this, the translator must keep asking the question, is what I wrote clear and readily understandable?

litotipi (line 7) - If you are not quite familiar with the subject of coal, you may want to first look up some of the technical terms in a scientific reference book and gain a general orientation regarding this subject.

i 3 cm (line 23) - While the English translation retains the decimal system, at times a client may require conversion to inches. Be sure to find out which system is required.

30°(line 29) - Degrees can be conveyed either by their symbol or by using the word "degrees." Whichever you use, be consistent, and don't switch back and forth without good reason.

90% (page 2, line 34) - Percentages can be conveyed by their symbol or by using the word "percent" or "per cent." All three are legitimate, but, again, be consistent.

ASSIGNMENT 4 - TRANSLATION

Calculation of the investments forecast by the Region of Sardinia

We have calculated the investments forecast for the implementation of the solution proposed by the Region of Sardinia, and following below are the considerations justifying the values presented:

The existing third of the Sulcis power plant: this group, the newest of the three, will be assigned to run on a mix of imported coal and Sulcis coal during the start-up phase of the mine, and then it will be revamped. For this power plant, we have agreed to what was planned by ENEL for the insertion of DeSox and DeNox plants which, because they were planned for imported coal, nevertheless require a proportionately lower investment due to the very low content of sulfur;

The new IGCC power plant: although our valuations of cost figures derived from the international market for thermoelectric and chemical components have brought us notably lower investment costs, in order to avoid useless arguments or protests, which we consider to be unproductive at this stage, we have decided to refer to the cost forecast for the first European power plant to run on clean coal, which Elcogas will build at Puertollano in Spain. Obviously, since the plants that we are going to propose on behalf of the Region of Sardinia are located in places that are perfectly equipped, being the sites of extant thermoelectric power plants and thus furnished with infrastructure and all common and general services, it is reasonable to forecast a cost reduction. And again, because we are proposing an investment realized by an electric company, and not by an international consortium that benefits from a series of contributions which is reasonably justifiable with prudent budgets, it is possible to forecast a further reduction in cost. In the final analysis, we believe that it is correct and prudent to indicate a specific cost of 2.32 million lire per installed KW for an IGCC plant with the capacity in this plan.

Revamping of the Sulcis power plant: the revamping consists of an extraordinary overhaul of the first two groups at Sulcis power plant, the insertion of a topping type combined cycle fed by synthetic gas produces from gasification of coal.

Revamping of the Portoscuso power plant: the overhaul is of the same type chosen for the Sulcis power plant, and it is planned for a later time since the plant is in better condition and is essential for supplying the adjacent electrolysis of aluminum (240 MW continuous). It must be noted that the overhaul presents very interesting technical characteristics on account of the particular design of the power plant, which is suitable for cogeneration.

What has been presented above is clearly illustrated in the following table:

2 **Scheme proposed by the Region of Sardinia**			
Table of investments	current solution	RAS solution	ENEL
Existing Sulcis plant 3	Billions of lire		419
New Sulcis plant	Billions of lire		2,288
New IGCC plant	Billions of lire	780	
Sulcis plant I revamping	Billions of lire	496	
Sulcis plant 2 revamping	Billions of lire	496	
Total phase I	Billions of lire	1,279	2,707
Sulcis margin of consumption	Billions of lire	492	
Portoscuso plant revamping	Billions of lire	1,006	
Sulcis plant 3 revamping	Billions of lire	496	
Total investments	Billions of lire	3,273	2,707
Investments forecast by ENEL	Billions of lire	3,415	-708

The configuration proposed by the Region permits the total consumption of currently forecast mine production, and it allows for its major growth, in total compliance with current and future (much more restrictive) legislation protecting the environment;

the specific investment per net installed KW is 40% lower than what is required by the plants planned by ENEL, by taking as a basis the costs presented by ENEL;

3 **Scheme proposed by the Region of Sardinia**			
Table of specific investments	current solution	RAS solution	ENEL
Existing Sulcis plant 3	Th.lire/KW		1,922
New Sulcis plant	Th.lire/KW		5,248
New IGCC plant	Th.lire/KW	2,320	
Sulcis plant 1 revamping	Th.lire/KW	1,740	
Sulcis plant 2 revamping	Th.lire/KW	1,740	
Portoscuso plant revamping	Th.lire/KW	1,796	
Sulcis plant 3 revamping	Th.lire/KW	1,740	
Total specific investments	Th.lire/KW	1,803	4,139
Difference in specific investment	Th.lire/KW	-2,336	

The energy produced by the configuration proposed by the Region of Sardinia is more than double that produced by the ENEL configuration. In this regard, it must be pointed out that the

IGCC plant is considered to be a generator of electrical energy with the same availability as a conventional plant. This is so because it will also be able to use a liquid fuel in the event that there are start-up problems in the chemical part during the first year of operation. Therefore, a capacity utilization coefficient of 7500 hours/year is assigned to this plant, just as forecast for the SARAS plant at Sarroch, where the gasification part can be considered to be of the traditional, familiar type since it consumes refinery TAR.

4 **Scheme proposed by the Region of Sardinia**

Table of energy produced		current solution	RAS solution	ENEL
Existing Sulcis plant 3	GWh/year	3,375		1,090
New Sulcis plant	GWh/year			2,616
New IGCC plant	GWh/year		2,016	
Sulcis plant 1 revamping	GWh/year		1,710	
Sulcis plant 2 revamping	GWh/year		1,710	
Total phase 1	GWh/year		4,267	3,706
Sulcis margin of consumption	GWh/year		1,169	
Portoscuso plant revamping	GWh/year		3,360	
Sulcis plant 3 revamping	GWh/year	340	1,710	0
Total capacities final phase	GWh/year	3,715	10,506	3,706
Difference in capacities	GWh/year	-6,791		-6,800

The specific consumption of an IGCC plant running on Sulcis coal is 1911 Kcal/KWh, while with imported coal this consumption drops to 1890 Kcal/KWh;

The dumps for ash produced by IGCC plants are not very complicated technically and of a lower class (Type 2A), insofar as they involve non-polluting materials since they are chemically and physically inert;

IGCC technology makes it possible to increase the value of the Portoscuso power plant by revamping it, while preserving the capital investment of a recent power plant and the jobs of its employees, and while obtaining new capacity at a cost lower than that for a new plant;

In the final analysis, this technology permits the genuine development of the Sulcis coal industry in the years to come while realizing high-yield electric energy production that respects the environment, exploiting the existing plants, and using a local asset of significant magnitude.

ASSIGNMENT 4: NOTES

General comments:

a. Financial Translation

In translation, there is a basic difference between translating financial subjects and other technical subjects, such as legal or medical. While it is relatively easy to master the methodology of working with most technical vocabularies, even if one does not have the technical or professional background of the particular field in which one translates, in financial subjects it is necessary to have at least a general knowledge of the subject. This may be due to the fact that financial terminology and concepts are not always as readily translatable as other technical subjects. The upshot of all this is that one should not be hasty to accept a financial assignment if one does not work in this field on a regular basis.

b. Style

This particular assignment consists of a text derived from coal mining. It represents an international organization involved in the development of coal mining. As with most major organizations, this corporation has its own "corporate style," which affects the way this material is translated. Normally, an organization of this magnitude employs its own translators, or uses outside translators on a regular basis, to acquaint them with its style. If called upon to translate this kind of text, be sure to familiarize yourself with the organization's style.

dalla Regione (line 3) - This could be translated as "by the Region" or "of the Region" or even "Proposed by the Region," based on the text in the opening sentence. The last option is tricky, since it adds a word that is not there, and should be used with care. The present translator chose "of" because it makes the translated text more clear, since "by" could imply that the region is doing the investing.

mix (line 7) and *revamping* (line 10) - It is a common practice around the world today to use English words freely in many technical subjects. Usually, the word has the same meaning as the original English, but not always. Do not render those words automatically, but make sure first that the meaning is the same.

valutazioni (line 16) - Valuation is a financial term, meaning calculating the monetary value of an undertaking or an existing financial entity. This is an example of using correct financial terminology, which is critical in the case of financial translation.

2,32 Milioni di lire (line 28) - Here the comma in Italian for numbers over 1000 changes to a period in English, while million is lowercase in English and uppercase in Italian.

Note about tables on pages 2 and 3:

In technical translation in general, and in financial translation in particular, one runs into a fair number of tables, charts, diagrams and so on. Thanks to computer technology, creating tables is immeasurably easier than it used to be in the "old days," when we used a typewriter on even (imagine that!) wrote by hand. One of the basic requirements for today's translators is to be familiar with the "create table," "create columns," and all the other text-related graphics of the various word processing programs, such as Microsoft Word, WordPerfect, etc. Some translators tend to take a shortcut and enter the table or box text in rows without the table or the box itself. This was acceptable some years ago when one did not have the time to design tables, but it is altogether unacceptable today. In our new environment of a highly competitive translation marketplace, the format and appearance of your work is just as important as its completeness and accuracy.

Another important observation about tables is the need to make them look as close as possible to the table in the source language, for comparison's sake.

Part Two

Translation: English into Italian

5/2 hours

ASSIGNMENT 1 - GENERAL

Welcome Aboard USS THEODORE ROOSEVELT (CVN 71)

The crew of **USS THEODORE ROOSEVELT (CVN 71)** extends a hearty "Welcome Aboard."

The officers and men are proud of our ship, and are eager to show it off. You will notice the imposing size and the state-of-the-art technology of this fine fighting ship. **TR**'s strength, however, is in the people who operate systems, prepare meals, launch and fly aircraft, and perform routine and not-so-routine tasks in this city of 5,500 men.

Forgive us if our pride in **TR** shows. We can't help ourselves. She is a great ship named for a great American.

Please enjoy your tour.

We are sincerely glad to have you aboard.

The LEGACY

On November 3, 1981, Secretary of the Navy John F. Lehman announced that the nation's newest nuclear-powered aircraft carrier would be named for the 26th President of the United States, Theodore Roosevelt.

In making the selection, Secretary Lehman stated, "Roosevelt personified the vigor and vision of America. He was one of the architects of our modern Navy, with complete faith in the necessity for the value of a strong Navy."

In 1898, as Assistant Secretary of the Navy, Roosevelt recommended a study of the military applications of Professor Samuel Langley's flying machine, the Aerodome. This was the birth of naval aviation.

Roosevelt became President in 1901, after the assassination of President McKinley, and was elected to a full term in 1904. In a show of U.S. sea power, Roosevelt dispatched the Great White Fleet around the world in 1907. He was aboard the flagship USS CONNECTICUT as the fleet returned to Hampton Roads in 1909.

MISSION/CAPABILITIES

USS THEODORE ROOSEVELT (CVN 71) is a key element of our country's forward deployed defense strategy. Tasked with maintaining open sea lanes of trade and communications, **TR** is capable of projecting air superiority to all points of the globe. Her tactical aircraft serve as outstanding instruments of peace. She also shares the task of replenishing ships at sea and performing a variety of non-combat missions such as the rescue at sea of people in distress and the transport of refugees and others in need of help.

Maintaining her equipment and men in the highest state of readiness enables **TR** to be capable of carrying out a wide variety of missions including anti-air warfare, anti-surface warfare, anti-submarine warfare and electronic warfare.

TR displaces more than 97,000 tons of water while moving day and night at speeds of more than 30 knots.

However, people make **TR** more than a mere mass of steel, cable and pipe. She is a floating city of 5,500 men from every state in the Union; officers and men with decades of naval service and those who just joined. It is the veteran enlisted man with gold on his dress blues and the "slicksleeve" 17-year-old, away from home for the first time, who provide her with heart and soul. These Sailors and Marines give her life.

Leadership, training and a sense of purpose blend each of these individual personalities toward one goal . . . being ready to exercise the power of **TR** in support of the goals of the United States.

TR hosted President Bill Clinton's first visit to a Navy ship, the sailed to the Adriatic as CVW-8 planes enforced Operation Deny Flight, the U.N. no-fly zone over Bosnia. In June, on the way to only her second port visit, **TR** was ordered to turn around and transit the Suez Canal to the Red Sea to participate in Operation Southern Watch, enforcing the no-fly zone over Iraq.

In November 1993, **TR** entered Norfolk Naval Shipyard (NNSY) for a Selected Restricted Availability (SRA). Heading back to sea on Apr. 14, 1994, it became the first nuclear carrier to complete an SRA ahead of schedule at NNSY.

TR received the Golden Anchor Award for the best reenlistment record on an Atlantic Fleet carrier, and its third Battle "E" for its outstanding record in 1993. Then on June 3, **TR** was awarded its second Battenberg Cup as the best ship in the Atlantic Fleet. Capt. Ronald L. Christenson assumed command of **TR** July 8, 1994.

The History of USS THEODORE ROOSEVELT (CVN 71)

USS THEODORE ROOSEVELT (CVN 71) is the fourth NIMITZ-class carrier. Her history began on Sept. 30, 1980, when a contract was awarded to Newport News Shipbuilding. Construction began on Oct. 31, 1981, when Secretary of Defense Casper Weinberger authenticated the keel laying of **TR** by initialing the first weld. Capt. Paul W. Parcells was named Prospective Commanding Officer in February 1984 and, that October the ship was officially christened. On Oct. 25, 1986, **TR** was placed in active service.

Capt. Dayton W. Ritt became **TR**'s second Commanding Officer on Oct. 3, 1987, and on Dec. 30, 1988, **TR** started her maiden deployment, which was also the maiden deployment of the first 10-squadron air wing, Carrier Air Wing EIGHT. **TR** was awarded the Battle "E" from Commander, Naval Air Force, U.S. Atlantic Fleet, on March 20, 1990.

On June 9, 1990 Capt. Charles S. Abbot became the ship's third Commanding Officer and on Dec. 28, **TR** and CVW-8 deployed for Operation Desert Shield. **TR** entered the war on Jan. 9, 1991, eventually launching over 4,200 sorties, more than any other carrier. CVW-8 dropped over 4,800,000 pounds of ordnance before the cease-fire on Feb. 28.

When Iraqi forces turned on the Kurds, **TR** and CVW-8 were among the first coalition forces in Operation Provide Comfort, flying patrols over northern Iraq. After a 189 day deployment, with 169 days at sea, **TR** returned to Norfolk on June 28, 1991. On Feb. 14, 1992, the ship won its second Battle "E." This was followed by the award of the Battenberg Cup for 1991 as the Atlantic Fleet's premier ship.

Capt. Stanley W. Bryant became **TR**'s fourth Commanding Officer on Aug. 27, 1992.

TR and CVW-8 began their third deployment March 11, 1993, teamed with the Special Purpose Marine Air Ground Task Force (SPMAGTF) to test the concept of embarking a multi-purpose Marine force in a carrier.

word count: 1023

ASSIGNMENT 2 - LEGAL

CERTIFICATE OF INCORPORATION
OF
ABC, INCORPORATED

*****

1. The name of the corporation is

ABC, INCORPORATED

2. The address of its registered office in the State of Delaware is 1234 Main Street, in the City of Essex, County of Sussex. The name of its registered agent at such address is the Registry Trust Company.

3. The nature of the business or purposes to be conducted or promoted is to engage in any lawful act or activity for which corporations may be organized under the General Corporation Law of Delaware.

4. The total number of shares of stock which the corporation shall have authority to issue is one hundred (100) and the par value of each of such shares is One Hundred Dollars ($100.00) amounting in the aggregate to Ten Thousand Dollars ($10,000.00).

5A. The name and address of each incorporator is as follows:

5B. The name and address of each person, who is to serve as a director until the first annual meeting of the stockholders or until a successor is elected and qualified, is as follows:

6. The corporation is to have perpetual existence.

7. Elections of directors need not be by written ballot unless the by-laws of the corporation shall so provide. Meetings of stockholders may be held within or without the State of Delaware, as the by-laws may provide. The books of the corporation may be kept (subject to any provision contained in the statutes) outside the State of Delaware at such place or places as may be designated from time to time by the board of directors or in the by-laws of the corporation.

8. The corporation reserves the right to amend, alter, change or repeal any provision contained in this Certificate of Incorporation, in the manner now or hereafter prescribed by statute, and all rights conferred upon stockholders herein are granted subject to this reservation.

9. A director of the corporation shall not be personally liable to the corporation or its stockholders for monetary damages for breach of fiduciary duty as a director except for liability (i) for any breach of the director's duty of loyalty to the corporation or its stockholders, (ii) for acts or omissions not in good faith or which involve intentional misconduct or a knowing violation of law, (iii) under Section 174 of the Delaware General Corporation Law, or (iv) for any transaction from which the director derived any improper personal benefit.

WE, THE UNDERSIGNED, being each of the incorporators hereinbefore named, for the purpose of forming a corporation pursuant to the General Corporation Law of the State of Delaware, do make this certificate, hereby declaring and certifying that this is our act and deed and the facts herein stated are true, and accordingly have hereunto set our hands this 10th day of September, 1990.

POWER OF ATTORNEY

For the granting of this Power of Attorney, Mr. Roy Sanders, appears in capacity of President of ABC, Inc., a company organized under the Laws of Delaware, who being duly authorized by the Board of Directors of the Company, hereby grants a General Power of Attorney, which according to law is broad and sufficient, in favor of Mr. Jack Smith, in order for him to act in name and representation of the Company to enter into negotiations with the Instituto Nacional de Información (hereinafter "INI") and others on behalf of ABC, Inc. and bind it with respect to the obligations which shall be performed in Venezuela in connection with a site management agreement to provide services to INI for maintenance, support, repair and operations of hardware and for the modification, support and operation of software for the modernization of the geographical information systems of INI.

In the event that Jack Smith becomes unavailable whether due to death, disability, illness or otherwise, then Joseph P. Roberts is hereby authorized to act on behalf of ABC, inc. instead of Jack Smith.

This Power of Attorney is valid for two (2) years from the date of signature.

WITNESS my hand and seal this sixteenth day of January, in the year of our Lord, one thousand nine hundred and ninety-six

.

word count: 686

<u>DO NOT</u> USE A HAMMER OR ANY TYPE OF IMPACT TOOL TO INSTALL THE "KLIP-LOC"

INSTALLATION OF BEDLINER "KLIP-LOC" FASTENER

1) Refer to figure 1 (attached). Locate the bedliner in the pick-up truck bed with the front edge of bedliner resting as far towards the front of the bed as possible. Figure 1 shows the bedliner in its relaxed position in the truck. DO NOT ATTEMPT TO INSTALL THE "KLIP-LOC" while the bedliner is in this position. You must enter the truck bed and using your foot, wedged in the bottom corner, directly under the "Klip-Loc" slot, exert force both down and towards the outside of the liner. The top rail of the bedliner should flatten and come to rest on the rail of the truck (as shown in figure 2).

2) Refer to figure 2 (attached). Insert the "Klip-Loc" where the arrow is shown (figure 2). Continue pushing on the bottom after you feel resistance, until the clip seats over the bottom edge of the slot with a "snap."

3) Refer to figure 3 (attached). Completed installation of the "Klip-Loc" is shown.

LODE-LOK® UNDER RAIL INSTALLATION INSTRUCTIONS

1. Position the liner in the truck bed: move to the left side of the truck and lift up on the left side of the liner, inserting and pushing the right side of the liner underneath the truck rail (Figure 2). Release and allow the liner to rest in the vehicle.

2. Move to the end of the truck bed and at a point left of center. Insert an 8 foot long 2" x 4" lever under the liner, to the left of center.

3. The liner must now be partially collapsed and folded for threading of the left side under the rail. To complete the installation:

Lift the end of the lever vertically approximately two (2) feet (Figure 1) and toward the right corner, collapsing and folding the liner so the front left corner can be positioned low enough to thread underneath the rail. Push down the front left corner as necessary.

4. After inserting the front left corner, thread the remaining portion of the liner under the rail while lowering the lever to a level position. Be sure the liner is pushed completely forward and is square in the truck bed so that the rear corner will slide easily under the rail.

5. Remove the lever and allow the floor of the truck bed to relax to a level position.

NOTE: Installation of the Lode Loc® liner itself does not require any screws. The offset under the rail tightens the liner to the truck bed so that no fasteners are required (Figure 3). The product design also provides a straight line both vertically and horizontally, making the liner workable from top to bottom when using a load locking device.

A cushion at the inserting end of the lever is recommended to prevent liner and/or truck bed damage during installation. A towel wrapped around the end and taped in place is sufficient.

INSTALLATION OF BEDLINER FASTENER USED WITH FORD FLARESIDE & CHEVY SPORTSIDE BEDLINERS

1) Position the bedliner in truck, insuring that the front rail is all the way forward in the bed.

2) Standing at the cab end, inside of the bedliner, with your foot on the inside corner of the bedliner directly below a slotted hole (approximately 1½ inches below the top of the bedliner). Drill a ¼ inch hole in the truck in the center of the slot. While remaining standing on the bedliner, push in the fastener until the head contacts the bedliner.

3) Move to the opposite side of the bed and repeat the procedure.

4) Repeat the procedure for the rest of the slots - a total of (6) times.

LODE LOC® BEDLINER TAILGATE PROTECTOR COVERS

INSTALLATION INSTRUCTIONS

1) Position the plastic tailgate protector over the metal pickup tailgate. Please carefully secure by clamping in position, then drill.

2) When drilling (¼") holes through the plastic tailgate protector and pickup steel body, we recommend a minimum of (2) holes at the top outer corners and (4) evenly spaced holes across the bottom. (The top is the upper portion of the tailgate - the bottom is at the hinge end).

3) Remove the plastic tailgate protector and re-drill the holes in the tailgate protector using a ⅜" drill bit.

4) Position the plastic tailgate protector on the steel tailgate so the holes line up. Push one fastener into each hole until the head of the fastener contacts the plastic tailgate protector.

5) The fasteners provided are plastic. They are designed to penetrate the aligned holes without backing out.

word count: 777

Value Portfolio

Creates Wealth Over the Long Term

Creating wealth over the long term with moderate risk is the primary objective of our Value Portfolio. And with an 18.6% compounded annual return (net of all fees) since its inception in 1974, it has a proven track record for meeting client goals and is Compu-Val's greatest success story.

In selecting stocks for our Value Portfolio, we follow a conservative investment principle, purchasing stocks that are inexpensive relative to the value of assets that the company controls. To do that, we calculate a **Value /Cost** ratio for each company, determining the market value of debt plus equity - the Value component - and comparing it to the company's inflation adjusted net assets - the Cost component.

In addition, we purchase only stocks of profitable companies with improving corporate performance as measured by cash flow return on investment (CFROI). Focusing on CFROI eliminates accounting distortions and gives a true "inflation adjusted" measure of corporate performance. The accurate comparisons we are able to make between companies lead to exceptional stock performance.

When evaluating a stock for purchase, we look for firms that combine low debt and financial strength. We favor companies with high quality products or services, particularly in niche markets, that offer attractive long-term opportunities. In addition, we buy companies that grow at a sustainable rate and focus on core businesses.

Portfolio holdings are monitored daily and review each week by Compu-Val's investment professionals. When a stock's market price reaches our goal, we sell. When a stock has a loss of 15% or more versus average cost, it is reviewed by our Investment Committee.

Fixed Income Portfolio

Minimizes Risk for Conservative Investors

Our Fixed Income Portfolio was established in 1984 to provide an attractive option for more conservative, risk-averse investors. It is designed to obtain the maximum return consistent with limited principal fluctuations and minimum credit risk. With a compounded annual return rate of 9.6% (net of fees) since its inception, our Fixed Income Portfolio has provided investors with consistent and positive results each yea. Investments are limited to Government bonds and corporate debt instruments rated "A" or better by Standard and Poor's/Moody bond rating services. Maturities are staggered, with the average portfolio maturing in 6 years or less. Investments are chosen based on our analysis of premiums for risk taken versus risk-free Government securities.

word count: 395

Benvenuti a bordo
USS THEODORE ROOSEVELT (CVN 71)

L'equipaggio della **USS THEODORE ROOSEVELT (CVN 71)** porge un caldo "Benvenuti a bordo".

Gli ufficiali e l'equipaggio sono orgogliosi di questa nave e desiderano farvela vedere. Noterete le dimensioni imponenti e la tecnologia avanzata di questa ottima nave da guerra. Tuttavia, la forza della **Theodore Roosevelt (TR)** consiste sopratutto nell'equipagio che fa funzionare i sistemi, prepara i pasti, lancia e pilota aerei ed esegue le operazioni sia di routine che speciali in questa città gallegiante di 5500 persone.

Perdonateci il nostro orgoglio nel mostrarvi la **TR**. Non possiamo contenere il nostro entusiasmo. Si tratta di una gran nave che porta il nome di un grande americano.

Godetevi la vostra visita.

È veramente un piacere per noi avervi a bordo.

RETAGGIO

Il 3 novembre 1981, il Segretario della Marina John F. Lehman annunciò che la più nuova portaerei a propulsione nucleare del paese avrebbe portato il nome del 26° Presidente degli Stati Uniti, Theodore Roosevelt.

Nel prendere questa decisione, il Segretario Lehman dichiarò: "Roosevelt personificò il vigore e la visione dell'America. Fu uno dei fondatori della nostra Marina moderna, con la più completa fiducia nella necessità e nel valore di una marina forte."

Nel 1898, in qualità di Segretario della Marina, Roosevelt raccomandò lo studio degli impieghi militari della "macchina volante" del professor Samuel Langley, l'Aerodome. Questo segnò la nascita dell'aviazione navale.

Roosevelt divenne Presidente nel 1901, dopo l'assassinio del Presidente McKinley, e fu poi eletto alla carica nel 1904. Per mostrare al mondo la potenza sul mare degli Stati Uniti, nel 1907 mandò in missione intorno al mondo la "Great White Fleet" (Grande Flotta Bianca). Egli si trovava a bordo della nave ammiraglia USS CONNECTICUT quando la flotta ritornò ad Hampton Roads nel 1909.

CAPACITÀ DI MISSIONE

La **USS THEODORE ROOSEVELT (CVN 71)** è un fattore chiave della strategia di primo impiego per la difesa del nostro paese. Con il compito di mantenere aperte le vie marittime per il commercio e le comunicazioni, la **TR** ha la capacità di impiegare la sua superiorità aerea in qualsiasi punto del globo. I suoi aerei tattici servono da efficace strumento di pace. Partecipa inoltre al compito di rifornire navi in alto mare e di eseguire diverse missioni non belliche. Quali il salvataggio in alto mare di chi si trova in pericolo e il trasporto di rifugiati e di altre persone bisognose di aiuto.

Il mantenimento di equipaggio e attrezzature nello stato più elevato di preparazione all'azione dà alla **TR** la possibilità di eseguire una gran varietà di missioni, tra cui guerra antiaerea, guerra anti-superficie, guerra anti-sommergibili e guerra elettronica.

La **TR** ha un dislocamento di oltre 88.000 tonnellate e una velocità di spostamento sia diurno che notturno di oltre 30 nodi.

Tuttavia, il nostro equipaggio, rendono la **TR** qualcosa di più di una semplica massa di acciaio, cavi e tabazioni. La nave è un città galleggiante di 5500 uomini provenienti da ogni stato d'America; ufficiali e marinai con decenni di esperienza navale o che si sono arruolati di recente. Sono sia il marinaio veterano con le strisce dorate sulla manica blu della sua uniforme che il diciassettenne con la manica tutta blu, per la prima volta lontano da casa, che costituiscono il cuore e l'anima della nave. Questi marinai e "Marines" le danno vita.

Il comando, l'addestramento e la consapevolezza di un fine da raggiungere fondono tutti questi individui diversi verso un unico scopo ... quello di essere preparati a impiegare la potenza della **TR** in appoggio dei fini degli Stati Uniti.

La **TR** ospitò la prima visita del Presidente Clinton a una nave della Marina, quindi salpò per l'Adriatico dove gli aerei della CVW-8 misero in atto l'Operazione "Deny Flight" (divieto di volo), la zona di divieto di volo sopra la Bosnia. In giugno, mentre era diretta verso il suo secondo ancoraggio in porto, fu ordinato alla **TR** di ritornare indietro e passare il Canale di Suez verso il Mar Rosso allo scopo di partecipare all'operazione "Southern Watch" (Controllo del Sud), per far rispettare la zona di divieto di volo sopra l'Iraq.

Nel novembre del 1993, la **TR** entrò nei cantieri navali Norfolk Navy Shipyard (NNSY) per Disponibilità ristretta selezionata (SRA). Salpò di nuovo il 14 aprile 1994, diventando la prima portaerei nucleare ad aver completato uno SRA in anticipo sul programma presso il NNSY.

La **TR** ha ricevuto il riconoscimento Ancora d'oro per aver avuto il miglior record di riarruolamento su una portaerei della Flotta atlantica e il suo terzo riconoscimento di battaglia "E" per il suo record di eccellenza nel 1993. Poi, il 3 giugno, la **TR** ricevette per la seconda volta il riconoscimento della Coppa di Battenberg quale migliore nave della Flotta atlantica. L'8 giugno 1994, il Capitano di Vascello Ronald L. Christenson assunse il comando della **TR**.

Storia della USS Theodore Roosevelt (CVN 71)

La **USS THEODORE ROOSEVELT (CVN 71)** è la quarta portaerei della classe NIMITZ. La sua storia si iniziò il 30 settembre 1980, quando fu assegnato la appalto al cantiere Newport News Shipbuilding. La costruzione si iniziò il 31 ottobre 1981, quando il Ministro della Difesa Casper Weinberger verificò l'impostazione della chiglia della **TR** siglando la prima saldatura. Nel febbraio del 1984, il capitano di Vascello Paul W. Parcells fu nominato Comandante della futura nave e , in ottobre, la nave fu battezzata ufficialmente. Il 25 ottobre 1986, la **TR** fu messa in attività di servizio.

Il 3 ottobre 1987, il Capitano di Vascello Dayton W. Ritt divenne il secondo comandante della **TR** e il 30 dicembre 1988, la **TR** iniziò la sua missione inaugurale, che era anche la missione inaugurale della prima suadra aerea da portaerei OTTO (CVW-8) del 10° squadrone aereo. Il 20 marzo 1990 fu assegnato alla **TR** il riconoscimento di battaglia "E" dal Comandante della Forza aerea navale, Flotta Atlantica degli Stati Uniti.

Il 9 giugno 1990, il Capitano di Vascello Charles S. Abbot divenne il terzo comandante della nave e il 28 dicembre la **TR** e la CVW-8 furono impiegati per l'Operazione "Desert Shield" per la guerra nel Golfo Persico. La **TR** entrò in guerra il 9 gennaio 1991, dove lanciò oltre 4200 sortite, più di qualsiasi altra portaerei. La CVW-8 lanciò oltre 2175 tonnellate di materiale esplosivo prima della cessazione del fuoco il 28 febbraio.

Quando le forze irachene attaccarono i Curdi, la **TR** e la CVW-8 furono tra le prime forze della coalizione nell'operazione militare "Provide Comfort" (fornitura di assistenza), eseguendo voli di pattugliamento sull'Iraq settentrionale. Dopo 189 giorni di missione, di cui 169 passati in mare, la **TR** ritornò a Norfolk il 28 giugno 1991. Il 14 febbraio 1992, la nave conseguì il secondo riconoscimento di battaglia "E". Questo fu seguito dal riconoscimento della Coppa di Battenberg quale prima nave della Flotta atlantica.

Il 27 agosto 1992, il capitano di vascello Stanley W. Bryant divenne il quarto comandante della **TR**.

La **TR** e la CVW-8 iniziarono la loro terza missione l'11 marzo 1993, in coordinazione con la Forza per impieghi speciali marittimi, terrestri, aerei (SPMAGTR) per callaudare il piano di imbarcare una forza di Marine pluriuso du una portaerei.

ASSIGNMENT 1: NOTES

General Comment:

This text has a very specific format, with well defined sections, bolded text and large headings and subheadings. The reason being, this is a pamphlet distributed by the U.S. Navy as a gesture of good will whenever a Navy ship docks in a foreign port. The translator of this kind of technical, specially formatted text makes sure that the translation text reflects the physical format of the original as much as possible.

While this text is written in general terms to be read by the general public, there are sections with some navy-specific terminology, which may require a certain amount of research and looking up. There are good English-Italian technical and naval dictionaries, which can be of great help with this kind of text.

The crew (line 6), and *The officers and men* (line 7) - The Italian translators uses the same Italian word for "crew" and "men." Actually the wording in the original is somewhat strange, since they may also be women on board, and since officers also include men. Be it as it may, the "men" are indeed the crew.

show it off (line 8) - This is American slang. Slang is often difficult to translate into another language, which may or may not have a slang equivalent for exactly the same term. Here is where translators have to show their resourcefulness and creativity.

5,500 men (line 11) - Be sure to change the comma in the English in numbers over 1000 to a period, or omit it altogether.

26th President (line 24) - Capitalization in English does not always follow in Italian. Be careful to follow the correct Italian conventions in matters of capitalization.

Great White Fleet (lines page 2, line 2-3) - This is the "official name of Roosevelt's Navy, and was thus left in English with the literal Italian translation in parentheses. See also *Deny Flight* (line 26) and *Southern Watch* (line 28).

97,000 tons (line 19) - Note that in the Italian translation this figure was converted into metric tons (88.000). In such cases it is important to check with the client regarding English and metric measurements and their conversion.

"slicksleeve" (line 24) - Here is another example of American slang, which the translator circumvented by simplifying the text. It is quite possible that this is the best one can do with it.

Marines (line 26) - In Italian "Marines" [*marinai*] means "sailors," so this separate branch of the Armed Forces was left in English in the translation.

no-fly zone (line 35) - This is an official American military term. Is there an Italian official equivalent for it? There may or may not be.

NNSY, SRA (lines 37, 38) - These acronyms were left unchanged in Italian, even though they do not follow the Italian words. Famous acronyms, like U.K. or U.N., have to be translated. These, however, would not make much sense in Italian.

ATTO COSTITUTIVO DI SOCIETÀ
DI
ABC, INCORPORATED

1. Il nome della società è

ABC, INCORPORATED

2. L'indirizzo della sede registrata della società nello Stato del Delaware è 1234 Main Street, nella città di Essex, Contea di Sussex. Il nome dell'agente registrato per la società presso tale sede è The Registry Trust Company.

3. La natura dell'attività commerciale e gli scopi che verranno perseguiti e favoriti dalla società sono di dedicarsi a qualsiasi atto o attività permessa dalla legge per cui le società vengono organizzate secondo le Leggi Generali sulle Società del Delaware (General Corporation Law of Delaware).

4. Il numero totale delle azioni che la società sarà autorizzata a emettere è cento (100) azioni ordinarie e il valore nominale di ciascuna di tali azioni sarà di cento dollari ($100,00) per un ammontare complessivo di diecimila dollari ($ 10.000,00).

5A. Il nome e l'indirizzo di ciascun socio fondatore della società è il seguente:

5B. Il nome e l'indirizzo di ciascuna persona che svolgerà le funzioni di membro del consiglio di amministrazione fino alla prima assemblea annuale degli azionisti, ovvero fino a quando saranno selezionati e qualificati i loro successori è il seguente:

6. La società rimarrà in esistenza in perpetuo.

7. Non è necessario che l'elezione dei membri del consiglio di amministrazione sia fatta per votazione scritta, a meno che non sia così stabilito dallo statuto della società. Le assemblee degli azionisti possono venire indette entro o fuori dai confini dello Stato del Delaware, a seconda delle previsioni dello statuto. I registri della società possono venire tenuti fuori dallo Stato del Delaware (in base alle disposizioni contenute nello statuto) nel luogo o luoghi che siano designati di volta in volta dal consiglio di amministrazione o dallo statuto della società.

8. La società si riserva il diritto di rettificare, emendare, modificare o abrogare qualsiasi previsione di questo Atto Costitutivo di Società, nei modi ora o in futuro stabiliti dallo statuto, e tutti i diritti conferiti con il presente atto agli azionisti sono sottoposti a questa riserva.

9. I membri del consiglio di amministrazione della società non saranno responsabili personalmente verso la società o i suoi azionisti per danni monetari per inadempienza ai propri obblighi fiduciari in qualità di membro del consiglio di amministrazione tranne che in caso di responsabilità (i) per qualsiasi inadempienza agli obblighi di lealtà verso la società o i suoi azionisti, (ii) per atti od omissioni compiuti non in buona fede o che costituiscano violazione intenzionale dei doveri di ufficio o violazioni intenzionali di leggi, (iii) ai termini della Sezione 174 della Legge Generale sulle Società del Delaware, o (iv) per qualsiasi attività da cui il membro del consiglio di amministrazione abbia ricavato un beneficio personale improprio.

NOI SOTTOSCRITTI, essendo nominati soci fondatori con il presente atto allo scopo di costituire una società in conformità alla Legge Generale sulle Società dello Stato del Delaware, stipuliamo questo atto costitutivo, e qui dichiariamo e attestiamo che i fatti affermati in questo documento sono veri e perciò apponiamo la nostra firma in data 10 settembre 1990.

PROCURA

Per la concessione di questa Procura, il signor Roy Sanders è comparso nella sua veste di Presidente della ABC, Inc., una società costituita secondo le leggi del Delaware, ed essendo stato legalmente autorizzato dal Consiglio di Amministrazione della società, con il presente atto concede la Procura generale, che secondo la legge sia estesa e sufficiente, a favore del signor Jack Smith, affinchè egli rappresenti la società a iniziare le trattative con l'Instituto Nacional de Información (qui chiamato "INI") ed altri per conto della ABC, Inc. e lo impegna rispetto agli obblighi che dovranno essere svolti in Venezuela relativamente all'accordo di gestione del luogo a fornire servizi all'INI per la manutenzione, il supporto, la riparazione e l'operazione dello hardware e per le modifiche, il supporto e l'operazione del software per modernizzare i sistemi di informazioni geografiche dell'INI.

Nel caso in cui Jack Smith non dovesse essere disponibile a causa di decesso, invalidità, malattia o altrimenti, allora Joseph P. Roberts con il presente atto viene autorizzato ad agire per conto della ABC, Inc. invece di Jack Smith.

Questa Procura rimane in vigore per due (2) anni dalla data della stipulazione.

In attestato di quanto sopra, ho sottoscritto e apposto il sigillo in data sedici gennaio dell'anno millenovecentonovantasei.

ASSIGNMENT 2: NOTES

Certificate of Incorporation (line 4) - This could be translated literally into Italian. The translator, however, changed this heading to reflect official Italian legal usage, namely, *Atto Constitutivo di Società*. This conveys the same idea as "Certificate of Incorporation," which is the legal act of establishing a corporation. It is highly recommended to have a good English-Italian legal dictionary handy when translating this type of text. It is also good, if you can manage it, to have samples of such legal documents in Italian. This, in effect, is a standard legal document for the incorporation of a business, and should be easy to do once you have the right format, terminology, and style.

ABC, INCORPORATED (line 12) - The name of the corporation remains untranslated, since the entire name is a legal entity, and to render it or any part of it into another language may create confusion. The same is true in the case of *Registry Trust Company* (line 11).

Registered office (line 14) - This is another good example of legal terminology, which requires careful translation. "Office" is translated as *sede*, or central location, rather than plain office, in keeping with the legal sense of the text. Another example is *breach of fiduciary duty* (page 2, line 2), where "duty" means "obligation" or "responsibility."

The nature (line 18) - Any number of words might be appropriate here, such as "type," "objective," and so on. *Natura* may or may not be the best choice.

lawful (line 19) - The sense of this word as used here is "within the law," or "allowed by law," rather than "legal," which is what the Italian translator conveys.

General Corporation Law of Delaware (line 19-20) - Here the text is translated into Italian, with the English original provided in parentheses, to allow the reader to have the source reference, in case there is a need to look up this particular law, which is quite common in the case of dealing with legal documents.

($100.00), ($10,000.00) (lines 23, 24) - The use of commas in Italian for decimals, and periods for numbers in the 1000s, replacing the period or comma, respectively, in English, is a common source of translation mistakes. Be particularly aware of numbers, which many translators tend to treat too lightly.

provide (line 34) - The word *provide* has many possible translations, since it has many synonyms. As we have explained before regarding avoiding being too literal, however, we should, in translating this term, look to the essence of what is being conveyed, that is, the laws *provide* really means the laws *convey*, or *establish*. A law does not literally *provide* anything but rather states, establishes, posits etc.

amend, alter, change (page 2, line 1) - These all being synonyms, you have to be especially careful in picking the right ones. Sound judgment combined with a good dictionary is what this text requires.

Power of Attorney (line 17) - *"mandato di procura"* is the full translation of this legal term. Here again the Italian legal usage is what determines good translation, not the definition found in the dictionary. Your attention is drawn to the fact that such terms as "attorney," "prosecutor," "defense attorney" and all other references to the offices and functions of lawyers often cause problems in translation, since the functions of attorneys in different countries differ quite substantially. Be sure to use the correct Italian equivalent in each case.

in the year of our Lord (line 34) - In Italian, a date standing alone is assumed to be A.D., even in a legal document.

Note: *At the end of the original document, it mentions that there is a seal. Many of these sorts of documents have seals, stamps, franks, and signatures which have to be translated as well. You must refer to the position of the item on the page, followed by the translation, and enclose the whole item in brackets. For example: [seal in bottom left hand corner: signature, September 17, 1967] on the page where the seal appears.*

NONUSARE UN MARTELLO O ALTRO TIPO DI ATTREZZO A IMPATTO PER INSTALLARE IL"KLIP-LOC"

INSTALLAZIONE DI BLOCCA-RIVESTIMENTI "KLIP-LOC" NEI RIVESTIMENTI DEI PIANALI DI AUTOCARRI

1) Fare riferimento alla figura (allegata). sistemare il rivestimento nel pianale dell'autocarro da collettame con il lato anteriore del rivestimento appoggiato il più vicino possibile alla parte anteriore del pianale. La Figura 1 monstra il rivestimento per pianale appena appoggiato nell'autocarro, NON CERCARE DI INSTALLARE IL "KLIP-LOC" mentre il rivestimento si trova in questa posizione. Si deve salire sul pianale dell'autocarro e inserire un piede nell'angolo in basso, direttamente sotto la fesura del "Klip-Loc", facendo forza verso il basso e l'esterno del rivestimento. il bordo superiore del rivestimento deve appiattirsi e appoggiarsi al bordo dell'autocarro (come illustrato nella Figura 2).

2) Fare riferimento alla figura 2 (allegata). Inserire il "Klip-Loc" nella fessura come illustrato. Con il pollice premere la parte inferiore del "Klip-Loc" dove sitrova la freccia (figura 2). Continuare a premere su questa parte dopo che si comincia ad avvertire resistenza finchè il fermo non si fissa con uno scatto sul bordo inferiore della fessura.

3) Fare riferimento alla figura 3 (allegata), che illustra l'installazione completa del "Klip-Loc".

ISTRUZIONI PER L'INSTALLAZIONE SOTTO IL BORDO DETTA FIANCATA DEI LODE-LOC®

1. Posizionare il rivestimento nel pianale nell'autocarro: spostarsi sul lato sinistro dell'autocarro e sollevare il lato sinistro del rivestimento, inserendo e spingendo il lato destro del rivestimento sotto il bordo della fiancata dell'autocarro (Figura 2). lasciare andare il rivestimento in modo che si appoggi sul pianale del veicolo.

2. Spostarsi verso il fondo del pianale dell'autocarro e in un punto a sinistra del centro, inserire sotto il rivestimento una leva lunga 2,4 metri (8') e di 4x10 cm (2x4"), sulla sinistra rispetto al centro.

3. Il rivestimento deve ora essere parzialmente sgonfiato e ripiegato per venire infilato sotto il bordo della fiancata del lato sinistro. Per completare l'installazione:

   Sollevare verticalmente l'estremità della leva di circa 60 cm (2') (Figura 1) e tenendo sempre fermo l'angolo posteriore sinistro, ruotare la leva e il rivestimento verso l'angolo destro sgonfiando e ripiegando il rivestimento in modo che l'angolo anteriore sinistro possa venire posizionato abbastanza in basso da poter venire infilato sotto il bordo della fiancata. Spingere in basso l'angolo anteriore sinistro secondo il bisogno.

4. Dopo avere inserito l'angolo anteriore sinistro, infilare la parte rimanente del rivestimento sotto il bordo della fiancata abbassando allo stesso tempo la leva in posizione orizzontale. Accertarsi che la parte anteriore del rivestimento sia spinta completamente in avanti e sia ben allineata con i lati del pianale in modo che l'angolo posteriore si infili sotto il bordo senza difficoltà.

5. Togliere la leva e lasciar ritornare ilpianale dell'autocarro in posizione orizzontale.

NOTA: L'installazione del rivestimento Lode Loc® di per sè non richiede viti. L'essere forzato sotto il bordo fissa il rivestimento al pianale dell'autocarro in modo che non sono necessari dispositivi di fissaggio (Figura 3). Inoltre, la sezione del prodotto è ad angolo retto con lati perfettamente verticali e eorizzontali, in modo che il rivestimento è completamente utilizzabile in senso verticale quando si usa un dispositivo di fissaggio del carico.

Si raccomanda di usare una protezione all'estremità di contatto della leva in modo da evitare danni al rivestimento e/o all'autocarro durante l'installazione. Sarà sufficiente uno straccio avvolto attorno all'estremità e fissato con nastro adesivo.

INSTALLAZIONE DEI BLOCCA-RIVESTIMENTO USATI NEI RIVESTIMENTI DEI PIANALI DEGLI AUTOCARRI FORD FLARESIDE E CHEVY SPORTSIDE

1) Posizionare il rivestimento del pianale nell'autocarro, accertandosi che il suo bordo anteriore si trovi completamente in avanti nel piano di carico.

2) Stando in piedi dal lato della cabina, dentro il rivestimento del pianale, tenendo un piede nell'angolo interno del rivestimento direttamente al di sotto di una fessura (a circa 4 cm (1½") sotto la parte superiore del rivestimento), praticare un foro di 6 mm (¼") nell'autocarro al centro della fessura. Rimanendo in piedi sul rivestimento, spingere nel foro il blocca-rivestimento finchè la testa non entra in contatto con il rivestimento del pianale.

3) Spostarsi al lato opposto del pianale e ripetere il procedimento.

4) Ripertere il procedimento per il resto delle fessure, per un totale di sei (6) volte.

RIVESTIMENTI PER PIANALI LODE LOC® COPERTURE PROTETTRICI DI SPONDE POSTERIORI

ISTRUZIONI PER L'INSTALLAZIONE

1) Posizionare Il protettore di plastica della sponda posteriore sulla sponda posteriore di metallo del camioncino. Stare bene attenti a fissarla in posizione mediante morsetti prima di praticare I fori.

2) Quando si praticano i fori da 6 mm (¼") attraverso il protettore di plastica della sponda posteriore e la carrozzeria di acciaio del camioncino, noi raccomandiamo di praticre almeno due (2) fori agli angoli superiori esterni e quattro (4) fori equidistanti attraverso il fondo. (L'alto è la parte superiore della sponda posteriore - il fondo è il lato della cerniera).

3) Rimuovere il protettore di plastica della sponda posteriore e rifare i fori nel protettore della sponda posteriore usando una puntina di trapano da 9 mm (⅜").

4) Posizionare il protettore di plastica della sponda posteriore sulla sponda posteriore di acciaio in modo che i fori siano allineati. Spingere ogni dispositivo di fissaggio dentro ciascun foro finchè la testa di fissggio non venga in contatto con il protettore di plastica della sponda posteriore.

5) I dispositive di fissaggio forniti sono di plastica. Sono disegnati in modo che possano penetrare nei fori, una volta allineati, <u>senza</u> fuoriuscirne.

ASSIGNMENT 3: NOTES

General Comments:

Format:

This text consists of instructions for installing a bedliner for a truck. As such, they are arranged in sections and numbered paragraphs to make it easier for the user to follow. It is important in formatting the translation text and illustrations to follow the physical form of the original closely and accurately, so as not to lose this logical order.

Subject matter:

This text contains some very specific technical terminology, which cannot be guessed at, but rather needs to be as accurate as possible. Here a good dictionary of mechanical engineering and automotive subjects can be very useful.

Klip-Loc (line 9) - This is a brand name, hence it remains untranslated.

LODE LOC® (line 19) - This is another brand name, followed by the rights symbol, which can be found in your computer's word processing symbols section, and constitutes an important part of the text.

8 foot long (line 33) - The Italian translation converts the feet into meters, but provides the original measurement in parentheses. The issue of measurement conversion in technical translation needs to be checked with your client or end-user, to make sure you provide the right system.

FORD FLARESIDE & CHEVY SPORTSIDE (page 2, line 20) - These terms were too specific to be translated and properly understood in Italian. While they may not be a brand name, they come close to being one, and trying to render them in another language may cause the reader to miss the meaning of the item described.

Illustrations: In this type of document the illustrations are extremely important, and should be rendered as clearly and completely as possible. With the help of the computer's graphic functions one can reproduce these drawings and key in the Italian words. At a minimum, a neat "cut and paste" job, consisting of photocopying the drawings and pasting in the printed Italian words may do.

Portafoglio di Valori

Crea un patrimonio a lungo termine

La creazione di un patrimonio a lungo termine con un rischio moderato è l'obiettivo primario del nostro Portafoglio di Valori. E con una redditività annuale del 18,6% composto (al netto di tutte le commissioni), la Compu-Val ha dimostrato sin dall'inizio, nel 1974, un record eccezionale nel soddisfare le esigenze degli investitori e questo costituisce il suo maggiore successo.

Nel selezionare i titoli per il nostro Portafoglio di Valori, seguiamo principi di investimento prudenti, in quanto acquistiamo titoli non costosi relativamente al valore dei beni controllati dalla società. Per farlo, calcoliamo il rapporto valore-costo per ogni società, determinando il valore di mercato del debito più le passività patrimoniali - componente del valore - e lo confrontiamo con i beni netti della società conguagliati al tasso di inflazione - la componente del costo.

Inoltre, acquistiamo solo titoli di società redditizie con rendimento aziendale in via di miglioramento misurato dal flusso di cassa del reddito sugli investimenti (CFROI). Concentrandosi sul CFROI si eliminano le distorsioni contabili e si dà una misura effettiva "conguagliata al tasso di inflazione" del rendimento della società. I confronti accurati che riusciamo a fare tra le varie società danno per risultato un rendimento eccezionale dei titoli.

Quando valutiamo un titolo da acquistare, cerchiamo imprese che presentano una combinazione di basso debito e solidità finanziaria. Favoriamo società con prodotti o servizi di qualità elevata, particolarmente in settori specializzati di mercato, che offrono opportunità attraenti sulla lunga distanza. Inoltre, acquistiamo titoli di società che hanno un tasso di crescita sostenibile e un'enfasi su attività non diversificate.

I titoli del portafoglio sono controllati ogni giorno ed esaminati ogni settimana dai consulenti finanziari della Compu-Val. Quando il prezzo di mercato di un titolo raggiunge il nostro traguardo, vendiamo. Quando un titolo subisce una perdita del 15% o superiore in confronto al costo medio, viene esaminato dal nostro Comitato per gli investimenti.

Portafoglio a Reddito Fisso

Minimizza il rischio per gli investitori prudenti

Il nostro Portafoglio a Reddito Fisso fu costituito nel 1984 per offrire una desiderabile opzione agli investitori più prudenti, contrari all'assunzione di rischi. È pianificato in modo da ottenere la massima redditività possibile, con fluttuazioni limitate di capitale e rischio minimo del credito. Con una redditività annuale del 9,6% composto (al netto di tutte le commissioni) sin dall'inizio, il nostro Portafoglio a Reddito Fisso ha dato agli investitori risultati positivi costanti ogni anno. Gli investimenti si limitano ai buoni del Tesoro e alle obbligazioni di società con una quotazione di almeno "A" da parte dei servizi di quotazione delle obbligazioni dello Standard and Poor's/ Moody. Le scadenze vengono scaglionate, con un portafoglio medio che perviene a maturazione in sei anni o meno. Gli investimenti sono scelti in base alle nostre analisi dei premi per il rischio assunto a confronto con i titoli governativi privi di rischio.

Value Portfolio (line 3) - Phrases such as this occur more in the United States than anywhere else in the world. These are fanciful terms which are created in the business, advertising, and media industries, many of which seem commonplace in everyday life in this country, but which, in practical terms and at first sight, seem impossible to translate. The best way of handling this challenge is to try to analyze the author's meaning as best you can. This can be accomplished by not being too literal (which could result in an absolutely silly and meaningless phrase), but by thinking carefully about what the author is really getting at, and thus not straying from the essence of the text. In this instance, *Portafoglio di Valori* seemed to be the best approximation, which is sometimes all we can do, no matter how hard we try. One could also follow the Italian translation with the English original in parentheses, since it is a name of a "financial product," which the Italian reader should be able to refer to. This is **not** to be taken to mean that you have *carte blanche* to cover yourself whenever you are not sure of a translation by adding the original in parentheses, but in cases where the original term was a made-up, albeit proper, term, it is all right to do that to further inform the audience.

A similar case is presented by the example of "niche markets" (line 23), although this is not a proper name but a "catch-all" phrase that has meaning in the United States, although maybe not in other countries, even if translated as well as possible. So, once again, you need to examine the context and come up with the closest approximation of what the author is referring to, which in our present translation may not be the best interpretation, so you may want to try to improve upon it. Who knows? You may even coin a new term in Italian. . .

18.6% (line 6) - Here we turn your attention to both the fact that in decimals the Italian changes the period to a comma, and that if you use the percentage symbol you should stick to it, and not spell out "percent" or "per cent" the next time around. Be consistent!

compounded annual return (line 8) - This phrase, although perhaps coined artificially for purposes of public consumption, does not need to be analyzed in terms of the author's intention. A good commercial/business and finance dictionary can give you subject-specific words separately, if not in compounded (no pun intended) form, which will allow you to put together the best phrase you can come up with if no standard is available.

CFROI (line 18) - Since this refers to a subject-specific term, it does not make sense to translate it literally and make up a new acronym for it. instead, it should be translated first, possibly with the original in brackets to let the audience know that it "came from" somewhere else (i.e., you did not make it up), and then give the real acronym that will be used throughout.

Section 4:

Where Do I Go from Here?

After you have completed all the assignments, or at least those you have chosen to do, you have to make a major decision. If you have never translated for profit before, you have to ask yourself if you are ready to try your hand at soliciting for-profit translation work. If the answer is yes, contact one or two of the enclosed work sources (Appendix E) and apply for a test or a short assignment. If you have translated for profit before in a specific area, such as legal documents, and you feel you are now ready to venture into another area, such as medical translation, first try out some short assignments in that field, until you become comfortable with it. it is important that you develop a relationship with one or more translation companies in your own geographical area. There is absolutely no reason in this day and age for a translator, say, in Wisconsin, not to develop a profitable relationship with a translation company in Florida, and in time you may indeed find out that a certain company on the other side of the continent is your best source of work. But as a beginner, there are many advantages to interfacing personally with the staff of a translation company close to home. They can give you a great deal of practical advice, help you with the hardware and the software, and share other kinds of experience with you. There is an old saying: "A good neighbor is better than a distant relative."

If, on the other hand, you feel you are not ready to take the plunge, you may want to consider a translation course or study program. Refer to Appendix 4 in the book, and see if there is a program close to home you can sign up for. Or you may decide to continue practicing on your own.

Whatever you decide to do, don't give up too easily. If you do enjoy the challenge of translation, continue to improve you skills. Remember: Translation can be a full-time career or a very fulfilling and profitable sideline. It is definitely the kind of expertise worth having, no matter what else you choose to do with your time.

Appendices

APPENDIX A. REQUISITES FOR PROFESSIONAL TRANSLATORS

Any person who knows more than one language has the ability to explain a word or a sentence in what translators call "the source language" (the language you translate from) by using an equivalent word or sentence in what they call "the target language" (the language you translate into). This, in effect, is the beginning of translation. But it is only the beginning. It does not automatically turn a person into an accomplished translator. Along with the knowledge of the source and the target language, a translator must have an aptitude for translation. Some people are endowed with a talent for translation. It is not an acquired skill, like riding a bicycle. It is rather a talent, like playing the violin. Some people have it and some don't. It is not necessarily an indication of a lower or higher IQ. Nor is it an indication of how linguistically gifted one is. It is an inborn skill that enables a person to change a text from one language into another quickly and accurately, or, if you will, think in more than one language at the same time. If you possess this skill, then it behooves you to develop it and make use of it, because there is never an overabundance of good translators, and it is almost axiomatic that the good ones can always find either full-time or part-time work.

The **first** requisite for the working translator is a thorough knowledge of both the source and the target languages. There is no point in billing oneself as a translator if one is not fully familiar with both languages, or does not possess a vocabulary in both equal to that of a speaker of those languages who has a universi-ty education or its equivalent.

The **second** requisite is thorough "at-homeness" in both cultures. A language is a living phenomenon. It does not exist apart from the culture where it is spoken and written. It communicates not only the names of objects and different kinds of action, but also feelings, attitudes, beliefs, and so on. To be fully familiar with a language, one must also be familiar with the culture in which the language is used, indeed, with the people who use it, their ways, manners, beliefs and all that goes into making a culture.

Third, one must keep up with the growth and change of the language, and be up-to-date in all of its nuances and neologisms. Languages are in a constant state of flux, and words change meaning from year to year. A pejorative term can become laudatory, and a neutral term can become loaded with meaning. Thirty years ago the English word "gay" simply meant "joyous." Now it is used to define an entire segment of society. We once spoke of the "almighty dollar." Now as we travel abroad we may find out the dollar is not necessarily everyone's preferred currency.

Fourth, a distinction must be made between the languages one translates from and into. Generally speaking, one translates from another language into one's own native language. This is because one is usually intimately familiar with one's own language, while even years of study and experience do not necessarily enable one to be completely at home with an acquired language. The exceptions to this rule are usually those people who have lived in more than one culture, and have spoken more than one language on a regular basis. Those may be able to translate in both directions. There are also rare gifted individu-als who have mastered another language to such a degree that they can go both ways. They are indeed extremely rare. Given all of this, one should allow for the fact that while the ability of the accomplished translator to write and speak in the target language (i.e., one's native tongue) may be flawless, that person may not necessarily be able to write excellent prose or give great speeches in the source language (i.e., the language from which one translates). Then again, it is not necessary to be able to write and speak well in the language one translates from, while it is to be expected that a good translator is also a good writer and speaker in his or her native language.

Fifth, a professional translator has to be able to translate in more than one area of knowledge. Most professional translators are called upon to translate in a variety of fields. It is not uncommon for a translator to cover as many as twenty or thirty fields of knowledge in one year, including such areas as political subjects, economics, law, medicine, communications and so on. Obviously, it would be hard to find a translator who is an economist, a lawyer, a medical doctor, and an engineer all wrapped into one. In fact, such a person probably does not exist. One does not have to be a lawyer to translate legal documents. Many a professional translator has been able to gain enough knowledge and acquire a vocabulary in a variety of technical fields to be able to produce perfectly accurate and well-written translations in those fields. This is not nearly as difficult as it may seem, since most technical fields utilize a well-defined number of terms which keep repeating themselves, and as one keeps translating the same subject, they become more and more familiar to the translator. One must, however, have a natural curiosity about many different areas of human knowledge and activity, and an interest in increasing one's vocabulary in a variety of related as well as unrelated fields.

Sixth, an effective translator must have a facility for writing or speaking (depending on whether the method used is writing, speaking, or dictation), and the ability to articulate quickly and accurately, either orally or in writing. Like a reporter, a translator must be able to transmit ideas in real time, and in good understandable language. Translation is a form of writing and speech-making, and a translator is, in a sense, a writer and an orator.

Seventh, a professional translator must develop a good speed of translation. There are two reasons for this: First, most clients wait until the last minute to assign a translation job. As a result, they turn to a translator or a translation service with what is perhaps the most typical question in this business: "How soon can you have this job ready for me?" The professional translator has to be prepared to accept that long job with the short turn-around time, or there will be no repeat business from that particular client or from most other clients, for that matter. Secondly, translation is generally paid by the word. The more words one can translate per hour, the more income one will generate. Translating 50 words per hour can land a translator in the poorhouse. Serious translation starts at 250 words per hour, and can reach as high as 1000 words per hour using word processing, and close to 3000 words per hour using dictation (the author actually knows such a translator). High volume translators are the ones who will be the most successful.

Eighth, a translator must develop research skills, and be able to acquire reference sources which are essential for producing high quality translation. Without such sources even the best of translators cannot hope to be able to handle a large variety of subjects in many unrelated fields. Dedicated translators are the ones who are always on the lookout for new reference sources, and over time develop a data bank which can be used in their work.

Ninth, today's translator cannot be a stranger to hardware, software, fax, modem, the Internet, and the latest developments in all those media. Translation has become completely dependent on electronic tools. Gone are the days of handwriting, the typewriter, and all the other "prehistoric" means of communication. The more one becomes involved in translation, the more one finds oneself caught up in the latest high-tech developments.

Tenth, a translator who wishes to be busy on a fairly regular basis doing translation work must carefully consider the fact that certain languages are in high demand, say, in Washington or in Los Angeles, while others are not. Thus, for example, there is high demand for Japanese, German, Spanish, French, Chinese, Arabic, Russian and Italian in both Washington and Los Angeles, but not nearly as much for Bulgarian, Farsi, Czech, or Afrikaans. If your language falls within the second group, it is extremely advisable to also have language expertise in one of the languages of the first group, or to seriously consider whether your particular language has enough of a demand to warrant a major investment of time and effort on your part. One should always check and see what kind of a potential one's language specialty has in a given geographic area.

The above ten points are the essential criteria for developing a translation career. There are many other considerations, but none as important as these. If you feel that you can meet all of the above criteria, then you should continue reading this handbook and putting it to good use.

The Well-Rounded Translator

The main division in the translation field is between literary and technical translation. Literary translation, which covers such areas as fiction, poetry, drama, and the humanities in general, is often done by writers of the same genre who actually author works of the same kind in the target language, or at least by translators with the required literary aptitude. For practical reasons, this handbook will not cover literary translation, but will instead focus on the other major area of translation, namely, technical translation. High quality literary translation has always been the domain of the few, and is hardly lucrative (don't even think of doing literary translation if your motive is money), while technical translation is done by a much greater number of practitioners, and is an ever-growing and expanding field with excellent earning opportunities. This chapter discusses the characteristics of the well-rounded technical translator.

The term "technical" is extremely broad. In the translation business it covers much more than technical subjects in the narrow sense of the word. In fact, there is an overlap between literary and technical translation when it comes to such areas as social sciences, political subjects, and many others.

One way of defining technical translation is by asking the question, does the subject being translated require a specialized vocabulary, or is the language non-specialized? If the text being translated includes specialized terms in a given field, then the translation is technical.

The more areas (and languages) a translator can cover, the greater the opportunity for developing a successful translation career. Furthermore, as one becomes proficient in several areas, it becomes easier to add more. Besides, many technical areas are interrelated, and proficiency in one increases proficiency in another. In addition, every area breaks down into many subareas, each with its own vocabulary and its own linguistic idiosyncrasies. Thus, for example, translating in Arabic does not make one an expert in all spoken Arabic dialects, yet a knowledge of several of those dialects is very beneficial for the professional Arabic translator.

How does one become a well-rounded translator? The answer can be summed up in one word—experience. The key to effective translation is practice. Since human knowledge grows day by day, and since language keeps growing and changing, the well-rounded translator must keep in touch with knowledge and language on a regular basis. The worst thing that can happen to a translator is to be out of touch with the source language for more than a couple of years. What the rusty translator may find out is that new words, new concepts and new ways of using those words and applying those concepts have come into being during that period of "hibernation," and one's old expertise is no longer reliable.

Translation, therefore, is a commitment one makes not for a limited period of time, but rather long-term. It is to be assumed that anyone who becomes a translator is the kind of person who loves words and loves the challenge of using words effectively and correctly. Such a person will not become an occasional translator, but will make translation a lifelong practice.

Good and Bad Translation Habits

The accomplished translator can develop good as well as bad habits. Starting with the bad, we have already pointed out one—losing touch with the source language for long periods of time. Another bad habit is taking illegitimate shortcuts while translating. There are several types of such shortcuts. The most typical is failing to look up a word one is really not sure how to translate. Being ninety percent sure of a word's meaning is not good enough in professional translation. If one is not sure of a word's meaning, even after all available means have been exhausted, then one must put in a translator's note to that effect, or make it known in some other way that there is a problem with translating that particular word. Anything less would be deceptive.

Another illegitimate shortcut is summarizing a paragraph instead of providing a *full* translation. There is such a thing as summary translation of a paragraph or a document. If a summary is called for, then this is precisely what the translator is expected to provide. But the most common form of translation is what's known in the business as a verbatim translation, which is a full and complete rendition of the source text. When verbatim translation is ordered, anything less than a full translation is an illegitimate shortcut. Unfortunately, some translators tend to overlook this from time to time, especially when they undertake more work than they can accomplish by a given deadline, and decide to summarize rather than miss that deadline.

Perhaps the worst habit for a translator is to decide at a certain point in time that his or her knowledge of either the source or the target language is so good that it cannot possibly stand any improvement. The moment one stops growing linguistically, one is no longer on the cutting edge of one's profession. The good translator is a perennial language student, always eager and willing to learn more and to keep up with the latest.

As for good habits, the most important, perhaps, are the ones we obtain by reversing the above-mentioned bad habits. But there are many more. One excellent habit is to read professional literature in the field one will be called upon to translate in with reasonable frequency. One good example is *Scientific American*, which can help anyone who translates subjects of science and technology to learn the style or styles used in scientific writing. People who work in the field of translating business documents should definitely read business periodicals, not the least of which is *The Wall Street Journal*. One does not have to be a scientist to translate scientific articles, or have a business degree to translate business documents, but a general understanding of the subject goes a long way towards providing an accurate translation of the subject.

Another excellent habit is to translate not only for profit but also for enjoyment and experience. Most people, unfortunately, are not so taken with their daily work that they would want to continue doing it after hours for fun or practice. But an accomplished translator is someone who will on occasion translate simply for the sake of sharpening his or her skill, or accept a very small fee because of personal commitment to the subject matter, or because of a personal interest. This writer, for example, enjoys translating poetry because of the challenge of doing what is perhaps the most difficult type of translation, and, quite simply, because of the enjoyment of poetry.

Yet another good habit is always to be on the lookout for dictionaries. Many dictionaries are hard to find, and are available in few places. This writer in all his travels across the United States and abroad always stops in bookstores to look for dictionaries. One can also order dictionaries from bookstores and from publishers, but then one has to know what to order and from whom. (See Appendix 2).

The last good habit I would like to mention is the practice of compiling word lists and building a reference library. Dictionaries do not have all the words and terms a translator needs, nor do they contain all the information which specialized references may have. There are aids for translators put out by certain organizations, and there is professional literature in every field. In recent years there has been a growing awareness of the need for terminology management (see Chapter 9), and with the constant advances in computer technology databases have been proliferating, making the work of the translator much easier than ever before. Good references are worth their weight in gold when they are needed for a specific translation, and over time the experienced translator develops an extensive library of glossaries which become essential for any translation assignment.

APPENDIX B: TRANSLATION TECHNIQUES

The first five chapters of this books were devoted to the background, requisites, and problems of translation in general and certain languages in particular. In other words, the more theoretical aspects of translation. The rest of this handbook is devoted to the "nuts and bolts" of the translation craft and business, the techniques, equipment, tools, and so on. The last part of the book consists of appendices which provide extensive information on dictionaries and where to find them, current sources of translation work, translation study programs, accreditation for translators, and publications of interest to translators. The present chapter discusses the best ways to handle translation assignments.

Preliminary Considerations

You are given a text to translate. Before you commit yourself to doing any work on it, you must ask yourself a few preliminary questions. They are:

1. Is the text legible?
2. Am I familiar enough with the subject to tackle it?
3. Do I have the linguistic resources (dictionaries, human contacts) to decipher unfamiliar words?
4. Is the text complete, or are there any missing parts?
5. Can I do it within the requested timeframe?
6. Do I have a good reason for doing it (doing it as a learning experience, or because you enjoy it, or to help a friend, or because you are properly compensated for doing it)?

Once you have answered all the above questions to your own satisfaction, you are ready to proceed with the translation.

Effective Approaches

There is no single effective approach to translation, and over time translators develop personal techniques that enhance the quality and the speed of their translation. No one set of rules applies equally to everyone, but there are certain methods and means of translation which can help almost any translator achieve greater accuracy and output. The following is a review of some of the key techniques that are becoming almost universal among professional translators.

The first and foremost question a translator must deal with today is what kind of equipment to use in the process of translating. In the days of the pen and the typewriter this question was much less crucial. Today, however, translation has become almost totally dependent on computers, for several good reasons: (a) Word processing allows far greater flexibility in producing text than any other contemporary means. The output of most translators has been tripled and quadrupled through the use of computers; (b) Computers allow text to be stored on a disk and reprinted or modified later on, a function which is invaluable in the translation field; (c) Clients nowadays are getting used to asking for translation on disk, since it allows them to edit, reprint, modify and enhance the physical appearance of a document; (d) If more than one translator is involved in a given translation project, the text from the various translators can be entered by an editor on one disk and equalized or manipulated as necessary, without having to redo any particular portion thereof.

In addition, it is becoming more common every day to use electronic means such as a modem, fax or e-mail to transmit and receive text. These tools are no longer a luxury. Their cost has been coming down, and more and more translators are acquiring them. Many people today are saying they cannot imagine how translators were ever able to manage without them. The answer is very simple: manage we did, but it took us ten days to two weeks to do what we can now receive, translate and deliver in two or three days.

The next question when approaching a translation assign-ment is: Am I qualified to do this particular translation? Only an honest answer will do. If one is not sure, then chances are one should not tackle that particular task. One must feel confident about a particular assignment if the results are to be satisfactory. The exception to this rule is a case where a client cannot find anyone else to do that particular job, and for some good reason is either willing to take a chance or to receive less than a complete and fully accurate rendition. In such a case it should be made clear between translator and client that the translation is not legally binding.

Once the commitment is made to proceed with the job, the translator will spend some time going over the entire document—even if it is book-length—and do a realistic assessment of the following points:

a. How long will it take to translate the document?
b. What reference tools are needed to get it done?
c. What kind of preliminary steps are needed prior to the actual work of translating?
d. What special problems are related to the document, such as legibility of blurred or poorly copied text or difficult hand-writing?
e. Does the document contain text in a language or languages other than the main source language, and, if so, can the translator handle that language?

Regarding the question of time, one can do a quick estimate of the length of the document by averaging words per line, times lines per page, times number of pages. An experienced translator has a pretty good idea of the number of words per hour he or she can translate. This is an essential feature of undertaking a professional translation job, since most clients have tight deadlines and tend to give repeat business to those translators known for keeping to their deadlines.

As for reference tools, if, for example, one is given a document about telecommunications, one should make use of one's own resources in that field and/or borrow from other sources whatever one needs to accomplish the task.

Preliminary steps prior to actual translation can include a consultation with an expert in a specialized technical field regarding a difficult term, phrase, paragraph or concept which the translator does not feel comfortable with. Having access to such experts is one of the translator's most cherished assets. It can make all the difference in the world between a correct and effective translation and one that misses the main point of the entire text. Another preliminary step is a trip to the local, regional or even specialized library to do some research on the subject.

The problem of legibility should be identified *before* one begins the task, not after. Sometimes the problem may start in the middle of the document and be so severe as to render the translation of the first part useless. In that case, the translator may have wasted a great deal of time. Sometimes the problem is minor, and does not affect the overall outcome of the translation. In other cases, the client may decide to proceed with the translation and simply put the designation [illegible] (between brackets rather than parentheses) wherever a word or part of the text cannot be deciphered.

Unbeknownst to client and translator, when a translation job is first assigned, there may be portions of text inside the source document in a language other than the main language of the document. This can happen in commercial, scientific and scholarly documents. It even happens in Tolstoy's novel *War and Peace,* when the author starts using French instead of Russian. This too should be detected prior to commencing the translation work, and a decision has to be made as to: (a) Does that text need to be translated? (b) Can the translator handle it? (c) Is it necessary to assign it to another translator?

Once all this preliminary work has been done, one is ready to proceed with the actual translation work.

Depending on the particular text, one should either start translating at this point, or, in the case of a text containing highly specialized terminology which may send the translator on frequent trips to the dictionary, one should first go through the document and make a list of as many unknown or uncertain terms as possible, and then spend some time looking them up and making a word list. This technique saves a great deal of time, since once a list is completed it is much easier to sail through the text, and the time spent initially on making the list is very short compared to the time wasted on repeated interruptions to look up words. Moreover, by first mastering the more difficult terminology of the text, one gains a much better understanding of the subject and is certain to produce a better translation. From the very start, make it a habit to compile word lists and glossaries of subject-specific terminologies, and keep it in a computer database program for future reference. In time, these lists will become your most valuable translation tool.

One should also follow good work habits. Some translators, particularly those engaged in freelance work, tend to overdo it, especially during their "busy season," when they can generate a large income during a relatively short period of time. They will go for twelve or more hours a day, and before they know it they will start complaining of stiffness in the neck and shoulders, blurred vision, and fatigue. One should not translate more than eight hours a day. Six is ideal. Eight is tolerable, provided one takes a few short ten to fifteen minute breaks. Ten is pushing it. Over ten is definitely hazardous to your health.

Before you get ready to submit your translation go over it again, using the following checklist:

Omissions—did you fail to translate any particular word or phrase, or even paragraph?

Format—does your format follow the original (breaking into paragraphs, for instance)?

Mistranslations—did you mistranslate any particular word?

Unknown words—were there words you were not able to translate which you would like to explore further?

Meaning—did you miss the meaning of any phrase or sentence?

Spelling—did you misspell any word which the spell-check function on your computer did not catch?

Grammar—did you make any grammatical mistakes?

Punctuation—did you mispunctuate or miss any punctuation marks?

Clarity—did you fail to clearly convey the meaning of any particular part of the text?

Consistency—did you call something by one name and then by another without any good reason?

"Sound-alike" words—did you mistranslate a word because it looks or sounds like the word in your target language but in reality has a different meaning?

Style—are you satisfied with the way your translation reflects the style of the original text (for example, the original is written in a clear, direct style, while the translation sounds more complex and indirect?)

This checklist is by no means exhaustive, but it does cover the main areas a translator must pay attention to.

As was already explained, your personal computer is your best friend when it comes to translating, editing, and producing a final copy. One can learn a few basic commands, say, in WordPerfect or Microsoft Word, and start using the computer. But there is much more to software than entering, deleting and inserting text. The better acquainted with software you become, the more it will help you with translation. Learn how to do columns and tables, how to use special technical and scientific symbols, do graphic functions, use the spell-check and the thesaurus, create data bases for glossaries and for your own adminis-trative records, and you will tackle a great variety of technical text in many fields at a speed that will amaze you. Remember: speed in translation is the most important thing next to language proficiency. Without it you will not be profitable, and you will be overrun by the competition. With an established record of fast accurate translation you can write your own ticket.

After a few years of using the computer you may want to consider dictation. Personally, I prefer a mix of PC and dictation. When I have an unusually long job and not enough time to do it in, I may revert to dictation. Otherwise, I prefer word-processing. One could argue that by dictating one gets more done and earns more, but there are other things to consider, such as the cost of transcription, the need to edit transcrip-tion, and the better control one has over writing than speaking. Some of us are natural speakers; others are writers.

One continues to develop translation techniques over time. One of the most wonderful things about translation, in my opinion, is the fact that your mind is never idle, never in a rut, but rather always being challenged by new tasks, new subjects, new knowledge, and the need to keep up with new developments in language, with different fields of human knowledge, and with the events of the world. As a translator in the Washington area since the late seventies, I have found myself in the middle of world events, beginning with the peace treaty between Egypt and Israel in 1979, when I met Begin, Sadat and Carter, and, more recently, in my daily dealings with events in post-Cold War Eastern Europe, with a strife-torn Middle East, the famine in Somalia, the new North American Free Trade Agreement (NAFTA) between the United States, Canada and Mexico, and the growing involvement of the U.S. space program with the space programs of other nations. Very few people cover as broad an area as a translator. Every day we in the translation business find new challenges, and have to solve new problems. As a result, we are always developing new techniques and finding new answers.

APPENDIX C: TRANSLATOR'S SELF-EVALUATION

The following criteria were developed some years ago by a U.S. Government agency for determining the skill level of a potential translator whom that agency might have liked to hire. You may want to read this chapter carefully to try to make an honest determination as to where on this scale you find yourself at this time. If you are below Level 2+, you need to keep practicing. If you are at Level 3 or higher, you can start doing some professional translating. After Level 4 you are ready for some serious translating, and at Level 5 you can start making a living as a translator.

Translator Skill Levels

Level 0
No functional ability to translate the language. Consistently misunderstanding or cannot comprehend at all.

Level 0+
Can translate all or some place names (i.e., street or city designations), corporate names, numbers and isolated words and phrases, often translating these inaccurately.

In rendering translations, writes using only memorized material
and set expressions. Spelling and representation of symbols (letters, syllables, characters) are frequently incorrect.

Level 1
Sufficient skill to translate the simplest connected written material in a form equivalent to usual printing or typescript. Can translate either representations of familiar formulaic verbal exchanges or simple language containing only the highest-frequency grammatical patterns and vocabulary items, including cognates when appropriate. Translated texts include simple narratives of routine behavior; concrete descriptions of persons, places and things; and explanations of geography and government such as those simplified for tourists. Mistranslations common.

In rendering translations, writes in simple sentences (or clauses), making continual errors in spelling, grammar and punctuation, but translation can be read and understood by a native reader used to dealing with foreigners attempting to translate his/her language.

Level 1+
Sufficient skill to translate simple discourse for informative social purposes in printed form. Can translate material such as announcements or public events, popular advertising notes containing biographical information or narration of events and straightforward newspaper headlines. Has some difficulty with the cohesive factors in discourse, such as matching pronouns with referents.

In rendering translations, writing shows good control of elementary vocabulary and some control of basic syntactic patterns, but major errors still occur when expressing more complex thoughts.

Dictionary usage may still yield incorrect vocabulary of forms, although can use a dictionary to advantage to translate simple ideas. Translations, though faulty, are comprehensible to native readers used to dealing with foreigners.

Level 2
Sufficient skill to translate simple authentic written material in a form equivalent to usual printing. Can translate uncomplicated, but authentic prose on familiar subjects that are normally present in a predictable sequence, which aids the translator in his/her work. Texts may include description and narration in context, such as news items describing frequently occurring events, simple biographical information, social notices, formatted business letters and simple technical material written for the general reader. The prose is predominantly in familiar sentence patterns. Some mistranslations.
In rendering translations, has written vocabulary sufficient to perform simple translations with some circumlocutions. Still makes common errors in spelling and punctuation, but shows some control of the most common formats and punctuation conventions. Good control of morphology of language (in inflected languages) and of the most frequently used syntactic structures. Elementary constructions are usually handled quite accurately, and translations are understandable to a native reader *not* used to reading the translations of foreigners.

Level 2+
Sufficient skill to translate most factual material in nontechnical prose as well as some discussions on concrete topics related to special professional interests. Has begun to make sensible guesses about unfamiliar words by using linguistic context and prior knowledge. May react personally to material, but does not yet detect subjective attitudes, values or judgments in the material to be translated.

In rendering translations, often shows surprising fluency and ease of expression, but under time constraints and pressure language may be inaccurate and/or incomprehensible. Generally strong in either grammar or vocabulary, but not in both. Weaknesses or unevenness in one of the foregoing or in spelling results in occasional mistranslations. Areas of weakness range from simple constructions, such as plurals, articles, prepositions and negatives, to more complex structures, word order and relative clauses. Normally controls general vocabulary, with some misuse of everyday vocabulary still evident. Shows a limited ability to use circumlocutions. Uses dictionary to advantage to supply unknown words. Translations are understandable to native readers not used to dealing with foreigner's attempts to translate the language, though style is obviously foreign.

Level 3
Able to translate authentic prose on unfamiliar subjects. Translating ability is not dependent on subject matter knowledge. Texts will include news stories similar to wire service reports, routine correspondence, general reports and technical material in his/her professional field, all of which include hypothesis, argumentation and supported opinions. Such texts typically include grammatical patterns and vocabulary ordinarily encountered in professional reading. Mistranslations rare. Almost always able to correctly translate material, relate ideas and make inferences. Rarely has to pause over or reread general vocabulary. However, may experience some difficulty with unusually complex structures and low-frequency idioms.
In preparing translations, control of structure, spelling, and general vocabulary is adequate to convey his/her message accurately, but style may be obviously foreign. Errors virtually never interfere with comprehension and rarely disturb the native reader. Punctuation generally controlled. Employs a full range of structures. Control of grammar good, with only sporadic errors in basic structures, occasional errors in the most complex frequent structures and somewhat more frequent errors in low-frequency complex structures. Consistent control of compound and complex sentences. Relationship of ideas presented in original material is consistently clear.

Level 3+
Increased ability to translate a variety of styles and forms of language pertinent to professional needs. Rarely mistranslates such texts or rarely experiences difficulty relating ideas or making inferences. Ability to comprehend many sociolinguistic and cultural references. However, may miss some nuances and subtleties. Increased ability to translate unusually complex structures and low-frequency idioms; however, accuracy is not complete.

In rendering translations, able to write the language in a few prose styles pertinent to professional/educational needs. Not always able to tailor language to suit original material. Weaknesses may lie in poor control of low-frequency, complex structures, vocabulary or the ability to express subtleties and nuances.

Level 4
Able to translate fluently and accurately all styles and forms of the language pertinent to professional needs. Can translate more difficult prose and follow unpredictable turns of thought readily in any area directed to the general reader and all materials in his/her own special field, including official and professional documents and correspondence. Able to translate precise and extensive vocabulary, including nuances and subtleties, and recognize all professionally relevant vocabulary known to the educated nonprofessional native, although may have some difficulty with slang. Can translate reasonably legible handwriting without difficulty. Understands almost all sociolinguistic and cultural references.

In rendering translations, able to write the language precisely and accurately in a variety of prose styles pertinent to professional/ educational needs. Errors of grammar are rare, including those in low-frequency complex structures. Consistently able to tailor language to suit material and able to express subtleties and nuances.

Level 4+
Increased ability to translate extremely difficult or abstract prose. Increased ability to translate a variety of vocabulary, idioms, colloquialisms and slang. Strong sensitivity to sociolinguist-ic and cultural references. Increased ability to translate less than fully legible handwriting. Accuracy is close to that of an educated translator, but still not equivalent.

In rendering translations, able to write the language precisely and accurately, in a wide variety of prose styles pertinent to professional/educational needs.

Level 5
Can translate extremely difficult and abstract prose (i.e., legal, technical), as well as highly colloquial writings and the literary forms of the language. Translates a wide variety of vocabulary and idioms, colloquialisms, slang and pertinent cultural references. With varying degrees of difficulty, can translate all kinds of handwritten documents. Able to understand how natives think as they produce a text. Accuracy is equivalent to that of a well-educated translator.

In rendering translations, has writing proficiency equal to that of a well-educated native. Without nonnative errors of structure, spelling, style or vocabulary, can translate both formal and informal correspondence, official reports and documents and professional/educational articles, including writing for special purposes which might include legal, technical, educational, literary and colloquial writing.

APPENDIX D: ITALIAN TECHNICAL DICTIONARIES

General Dictionaries
Cassell's Italian Dictionary: Italian-English English-Italian, Rebora, P. New York: Macmillan 1982
Italian Encyclopedic Universal Dictionary, 1994
Il Nuovo manuale de stile, Lesina, R., 1994
Visual Dictionary (Italian-English/English-Italian), Corbeil, J.C., 1992
Sansoni-Harrap Italian-English/English-Italian Dictionary, 4 vols., Macchi, V., London 1991 *Extensive, expensive.*
HarperCollins Sansoni Italian Dictionary, Kramer, A.L.N., Rutland, Vermont: Charles Tuttle 2001
Dizionario Italiano Ragionato, D, Anna, G., Florence: Sintesi 1988
Grande Dizionario Hazon Garzanti, Garzanti Editore S.p.A. 2001 *English-Italian/Italian-English*
Il nuovo Zingarelli vocabolario della lingua italiana, Zingarelli, N., Bologna: Nicola Zanichelli 1983 *Italian-Italian*
La nuova enciclopedia universale, Garzanti 1982 *Italian-Italian*
Collins/Sansoni Italian Dictionary, Macchi, V., Glasgow/Firenze: Collins 1981 *Italian-English/English-Italian*
Dizionario della lingua italiana, Devoto, G., Firenze: Le Monnier 1980 *Italian-Italian Excellent reference.*
Prontuario dei termini politici, economici, sociali in uso in Italia, Ferrau, A., Roma: Zingarelli Editore S.p.A. 1974
Il Ragazzini (Biagi Concise Dizionario), Zanichelli, N., Bologna: Nicola Zanichelli 2007 *English-Italian/ Italian-English*
Streetwise Italian Dictionary/Thesaurus, McGraw-Hill 2005

Italian: Business and Related Fields
Italian Business Dictionary, Sofer, M., Ed., Rockville, MD, Schreiber Publishing 2006
Nuovissimo dizionario commerciale, Ragazzini, G. & Gagliardelli, G., Milan: Mursia 1992 *English-Italian/ Italian-English*
Italian-English/English-Italian Finance & Commercial Dictionary, Picchi, F., Zanichelli 1990
Dictionary of Commerce (Italian-English/English-Italian), Motta, G., Milan: Carlo Signorelli Editore 1978
Italian-English English-Italian Dictionary of Economics and Banking, Codeluppi, L. New York: i.b.d. Ltd. 2001

Italian: Law
Dizionario Giuridico, de Francis, F., Eng.>It.(based on British Law), It>Eng (based on American Law) 1996 *Very fine reference.*

Italian: Medicine
New English and Italian Dictionary of the Medical Sciences , Biology and Biotechnology , Italian - English and English - Italian / Nuovo Dizionario Enciclopedico di Scienze Mediche e Biologiche e di Biotecnologie Inglese - Italiano e Italiano – Inglese, French and European Publications 2003
Medical & Biological Dictionary (Italian-English/English-Italian), Delfino, G.: Zanichelli 1996
Italian-English/English-Italian Medical Dictionary, Petrelli, M.: Le lettere 1993
Italian-English/English-Italian Medical Dictionary, Lucchesi, M.,: Cortina Rafaello 1987
English-Italian Dictionary of Medical Phraseology, Marino, V. New York: i.b.d. Ltd. 1985
Dizionario medico, Lauricella, E., Firenze: Sadea 1961 *Italian-Italian*

Italian: Military
Military Dictionary: English-Italian, U.S. Government Staff: Ross & Perry 2002

Italian: Nautical
Grande dizionario di Marina, Silorata, M.B., Cava dei Tirreni: Di Mauro 1970 *English-Italian/Italian-English*

Italian: Technical
Technical Dictionary, Marolli,G., New York: ibd Ltd. 2001 *English-Italian/Italian-English Excellent reference, now on CD-ROM.*
English-Italian/Italian-English Technical Dictionary, Ragazzini, G., et al, Milano: Mursia 1983.
Dizionario tecnico, Denti, R., Milano: Ulrico Hoepli Editore 1991 *Italian-English/English-Italian*

McGraw-Hill Zanichelli Dizionario enciclopedico scientifico e tecnico, Bologna: Nicola Zanichelli 1998 *English-Italian/Italian-English*

APPENDIX E: SOURCES OF TRANSLATION WORK

There are three major sources of translation work in the United States: the government sector, the public sector, and the private sector.

The government sector includes the city, county, and state governments in addition to the federal government. All of them need translation work on a fairly regular basis, and all of them are worth contacting. It is not always easy to find the right person or office to contact, but perseverance does pay off. One good place to start your search is the procurement or contracting office of any given government entity. They usually know who in the system needs what, and they can often tell you whether they've heard lately of someone in the system needing translation. Again, you need to have a great deal of patience with these folks, who are not known for their alacrity.

The U.S. Government, or the "Government" with a capital G, is a huge source of translation. It is hard to put a dollar figure on it, but it cer-tainly goes into the many millions of dollars per year. Government translation requests come in three main forms:

a. Translation contracts. Various government agencies issue a re-quest for a bid on a one- to five-year translation contract. Those usually require several languages, and most freelancers cannot handle them on their own.To find out about those contracts, read the government publication *Commerce Business Daily* (found on line at http://cbdnet.gpo.gov). You may want to monitor the contract office handling the particular contract, and have them tell you (under the Freedom of Information Act) which company is awarded the contract. You can then contact that company and offer your services in your particular areas of expertise.

b. Translation requirements in a non-translation contract. The Government may need a company to monitor drug dealers who speak Spanish. It contracts with a company specialized in electronic monitoring. That company will then subcontract the translation portion of its prime contract to a translation company. Here again you can follow this process, and offer your services.

c. One-time translation order. The Department of Energy may need to translate a Russian book on power plants. It will look for someone who has a good knowledge of Russian and English, and experience in this kind of technical translation. They usually turn to a translation company, but they may also contract with an individual. This type of assignment is very hard to find, since the agency will rarely advertise what they call a "small purchase" (which to a freelancer can be quite big), and will instead contact an established translation company.

The **public sector** includes many organizations, academic institutions, foundations, and so on. All of them, at one time or another, need translation work. The question is how to find out who needs what and when. I wish I had the answer, but I don't. The same holds true for the **private sector,** which consists of commercial and industrial entities, law firms, and individuals.

All of which leaves you with the **translation companies**, who in effect act as a broker between you and the work sources. They develop many contacts, they bid on contracts, they advertise in the media and in the Yellow Pages, and they provide millions of dollars worth of translation work for freelancers every year.

The following is a list, arranged alphabetically, of translation companies. It is followed by a state-by-state regional index. A word of caution: not all of them are financially sound, and they do not always pay on time or treat freelancers with the professional respect they usually deserve. **Inclusion in the ensuing list does not mean in any way that we endorse any of the companies listed**. We leave it to you to check out any company you may be interested in, draw your own conclusions, and establish your own relation-ship with them.

The information contained in the following list is based on survey questionnaires sent to translation agencies. The amount of detail cor-responds to the amount of information given us by those agencies that responded and does not reflect any judgment on the editors' part as to the quality of those agencies. We have attempted to fill in as much inform-ation as we could for those agencies that did not to respond to our survey.

U. S. TRANSLATION COMPANIES BY LOCATION

ALABAMA
Huntsville Alamex Translation Service, FLS

ARIZONA
Mesa A Foreign Language Service
Oro Valley CyraCom
Phoenix Choice Hotels International
Tucson CyraCom International

CALIFORNIA
Alhambra Asian Link
Berkeley Accent on Languages, Avantext, Berkeley Scientific Translation, Okada & Sellin Translations, OSTrans LLC
Beverly Hills ABC Worldwide Translations & Interpretations, Translate4-me Inc
Brea InterSol, Inc.
Carmel Richard Schneider Enterprises
Davis Avant Page
Encino Bizzy Box, Eurasia International
Exeter Clark Translations
Glendale Atlas, Coto, Inline, Omega
Hollywood ISI
Huntingon Beach ATS
Irvine Global Language Solutions/The Russian Word, Tru Lingua
Laguna Beach The Language Connection
Los Angeles Better Communications, INAWORD, Lazar & Associates, LRA Interpreters, 1-Stop Translation USA, Paragon Language Services, Rancho Park Publishing
Manhattan Beach Executive Linguist Agency
Menlo Park JLS
Merced Kramer Translation
Monterey Language Line Services,
Newbury Park ComNet International
Oakland International Contact
Orange Continental Interpreting Services
Palm Desert CC Scientific
Palo Alto BioMedical Translators, Health Outcomes Group, IDEM Translation
Padadena ITW Interpreting
Redondo Beach Corporate Translations,
Sacramento International Translation Service, Language Dynamics
San Carlos Peritus Precision Translations
San Diego Certified Interpreters & Translators, Interpreters' Index.com, Multilingual Translations, Rescribe
San Francisco Amelise Inc., Auerbach International, Excel Translations, Health Outcomes Group International Effectiveness Centers, The Language Bank, LUZ, Rosetta
San Jose Communicaid, Hightech Passport Limited
San Mateo Avid Translations
San Rafael Eurologos-San Jose
Santa Clarita America Translating Services
Santa Monica Lazar & Associates
Simi Valley Continental Communications Agency
Studio City Always Ready Translation Services
Thousand Oaks NetworkOmni Multilingual Communications
Walnut MAGNUS International Trade Services
West Hills N.O.W. Translations
West Covina American Education Research Corp.
Westlake Village Agnew Tech-II, ComNet International

COLORADO
Aurora Asian Pacific
Boulder Language Matters

Denver BRIDGE-LINGUATEC, Continental Book Company
Englewood Liaison Multilingual Services, Syntes

CONNECTICUT
Farmington China Communications Consultants
Millford Gene Mayer Associates
Riverside The Language Center

DELAWARE
Newark Pacific Ring Services
Wilmington Back to Basics

DISTRICT OF COLUMBIA
Washington ADA Inc., Federal News Service, Language Innovations, LLE Language Service, Language One, Transemantics

FLORIDA
Altamonte Springs Monti Interpreting & Translation Services
Aventura Carmazzi
Bay Harobr Islands CITI Translation Center Inc.
Boca Raton NovaTrans Enterprises
Coral Springs Semantics Translations & Publishing
Ft. Lauderdale Allslavic Translation Services, Artra International, Babel Tower
Lantana All Global Solutions International
Mary Lake AccessOnTime, Wudang Research Associates
Miami Albors and Associates, American International Business Counsel, Expert Translators, Josef Sliny & Associates, Precision Translating Services, Professional Translating Services, Traducciones LinguaCorp, Trans Global
Miami Beach American Evaluation and Translation Service, SBF Translation Services
Orlando The Language Bank, Trans-Caribe, United Nations Translators & Interpreters
Plantation The Global Institute of Languages and Culture
Pompano Beach
Tallahassee RussTech
Winter Park Albors & Associates

GEORGIA
Atlanta ALTA Language Services, Atlantic International Translators, Internark language Services, Total Benefit Communications
Columbus Total System Services
Loganville 3DWord

HAWAII
Honolulu Babel Corporation
Makawao Origin - The Language Agency

IDAHO
Boise Elocale, Inc.
Eagle Northwest Translations
Emmett Morales Dimmick Translation Service

ILLINOIS
Chicago Atlas Language Services, ACCUWORLD, Advance Language Studios, Burg Translation Bureau, China Beacon, Eureka-Foreign College Evaluators & Translators, Cosmopolitan Translation Bureau, Global Languages & Cultures, Heartland Cross-Cultural Interpreting Services, Nelles Translations, Quintana Multi-Lingual Services
Darien Arabic Dialects
Elmwood Park Communicad
Glenview Argo Translation

Palatine Square D/Schneider
Peoria Caterpillar, Inc.
Skokie Lingua Communications Translation Services
South Holland Techno-Graphics

INDIANA
Indianapolis International Bureau of Translations, Language Training Centre Inc., Pangea Lingua

IOWA
Cedar Rapids MGE Lingual Services, OmniLingua

KANSAS
Kansas City JLR Global Communications
Overland Park Interpretations, Inc.
Shawnee Around the World

KENTUCKY
Louisville Languages Unlimited

LOUISIANA
Metairie Alpha Tech Communications
New Orleans McDermott International

MARYLAND
Bethesda Advanced Communication and Translation, Italian Translations Company
Columbia Translingua
Crofton Compass Languages
Frederick Welocalize.com
Germantown Transfirex Translation Services
Montgomery Village M^2 Limited
Rockville ALC Inc., Allworld Language Consultants, Multilingual Solutions, Schreiber Translations, Transfirex

MASSACHUSETTS
Acton WORDNET
Andover ArchiText Inc.
Boston American Translation Partners, Brigham and Women's Hospital, Community Interpreter Services, The Multi-Lingual Group, New England Translations, Translation3
Cambridge Linguistic Systems, RIC International, RIC International
Lowell Agencia internacional
Randolph American ESL
Middleboro Rapport International
Somerville Affordable Business Services
Sudbury Rapport International
Topsfield The Translators
Wakefield Transtek
Waltham COMSYS Services, Venturi Technology Partners
Winchester Cross Cultural Comm Systems
Woburn Cross Cultural Communications
Worcester Baystate Interpreters

MICHIGAN
Ada Alticor ,Inc.
Ann Arbor Japan-America Management, University Translators Services LLC
Bingham Farms Detroit Translation Bureau
Clawson Techworld
Grand Rapids Translations Unlimited, Voices for Health
Novi Suzuki, Myers
Plymouth Speak Easy Languages,
Southfield Bromberg & Associates, International Translating Bureau,
Sterling Heights Vital International Programs Inc.

MINNESOTA
Brooklyn Park A-Z Friendly Languages
Duluth Superior Translations, Toward
Minneaplis Accu Trans, APS International, Arthur International, Betmar Languages, Garden & Associates, International Translation Solutions, Mena's International Corp., Multilingual Word, University Language Center
Minnetonka International Language Services
Wayzata Inlingua Language & Intercultural Services

MISSOURI
Belton Transimpex
Carthage Leggett & Platt
Kansas City Language Link Corporation, SH3, Inc.
St. Louis Calvin International Communications, International Institute of Metro St. Louis, International Language Center

NEVADA
Henderson Worldwide Translations Inc.
Las Vegas CG Translations, Escalante Translations, eTranslations

NEW HAMPSHIRE
Bedford ABLE International
Nashua Eurotext Translations, TEXTnology

NEW JERSEY
Bedminster Ambassador Translating
Bridgewater Counterpoint Language Consultants
Carlstadt O'Sullivan Menu Corporation,
Clinton aiaTranslations, Atkins International
East Brunswick The Language Center
East Windsor Princeton Technical Translation Center
Lawrenceville Premier Translation Services
Marlton Translation Company of New York
Morristown Allen Translation Service
Parsippany Newtype, Inc.
Pennsauken A2Z Global Language Solutions
Princeton Bloomberg L.P., Telelingua International
Princeton Junction Telelingua
Randolph Newtype, Inc.
Ridgewood Inlingua
Roselle Park Cybertec USA
South Orange Auracom
Summit Inlingua
Weehawken CLS Communications
West New York Continental Communications
Windsor Princeton Technical Translation Center

NEW YORK
Armonk ME Sharp, Inc.
Brooklyn Bilingual Professional Agency, Eriksen Translations, GES Translation Services
Central Islip MTS Multinational Translating Service
Fresh Meadows Eiber Translations
Gansevoort Copper Translation Services
Great Neck Eiber Translations
Hartsdale Marion J. Rosley
Long Island City Legal Interpreting Services
Marlton Translation Company of New York

Medford Angora Business Services
New York City Alanguage Bank, Audio To Go, Bowne Translation Services, C.P. Language Institute, 800-Translate, EuroNet Language Services, Gazelle Localization Group, Geneva Worldwide Inc, Geotext Translations, InterNation, Inc., Interspeak Translations, Japan Communication Consultants, The Languageworks, Merrill Translations, Metropolitan Interpreters and Translators Worldwide, R.R. Donnelley, Rennert, Translation Aces, translations.com, Transperfect, Trustforte, WKI
Niskayuna All Language Translations
Poughkeepsie Accurapid Translation Services, The Language Service
Rochester Advanced Language Translation, Language Intelligence
Schenectady All Language Translations, Copper Translation Service

NORTH CAROLINA
Chapel Hill DTS Language Services, Global Translation Systems
Charlotte Avantgarde Translations, Carolina Polyglot, Choice Translating & Interpreting
Salem Lucent Technologies Global Translation
OHIO
Chagrin Falls M/C International
Cincinnati CinciLingua, Inc., Conversa Language Center
Columbus Access interpreters, ALTCO Translations, ASIST
Holland International Language Source
Pickerington World, Inc., 12281 Butterfield Drive NW,
Raymond Honda R&D North America

OKLAHOMA
Norman Language Company Translations

OREGON
Aloha LangTech International,
Beaverton Bruce International
Portland Certified Languages International, Lingo Systems, Pacific Interpreters, SARJAM Communications, Telelanguage
Wilsonville Pacific Dreams

PENNSYLVANIA
Abington ABS Translation & Interpreting Service
Ardmor Language Services Consultants
Carnegie NCS Enterprises
Elkins Park CETRA
Lewisburg Lexiteria
Melrose Park CETRA Inc.
Philadelphia ISI, John Benjamins Publishing, Quantum, Inc.
Pittsburgh Echo international, Multilingual Communications Corporation
Wayne Americlic
Willow Grove Language Services Associates
Wind Gap Affinity Language Services

RHODE ISLAND
Pawtucket Narragansett Translations & Interpreting

SOUTH CAROLINA
Columbia Certified Translation Services

TENNESSEE
Memphis TRANSGLOBAL
Old Hickory NiS International Services

TEXAS
Alief Word Magic Software
Austin Adams Globalization, Larisa Zlatic language Services, Phoenix Translations, Ralph McElroy
Dallas Accento, Accurate Spanish Translations, Garcia-Shilling International, International Translating & Typesetting, The Language Network, Liaison Language Center, OneWorld Language Solutions

El Paso Language Plus
Houston AE Inc. Translations, Airspeed, American Bureau, Crossword, IRU Language & Translation Services, Language Direct, MasterWord, TechTrans International, Translation Source, Word Magic Software
Irving Korean Consulting & Translation Service
Katy Crossword Translation & Interpreting
Plano American Language Technologies
San Antonio Barinas Translation Consultants

UTAH
Centerville TermSeek
Midvale Asian Translation Service
Ogden U.S. Translation Company
Provo MultiLing International
Roy DocuTrans, Inc.
Salt lake City CommGap International Language Services

VIRGINIA
Alexandria Alexandria Translations, JTG, N. Virginia Area Health Education Center, TRADOS
Arlington ASET, Comprehensive Language Center, Inlingua
Harrisonburg Linguistic Services
Herndon Cascades Technologies
McLean BBC Multilingual Translations
Reston Antiquariat Literary Services, PSC, Inc.
Triangle Albanian Translation Services
Virginia Beach Global Visions, The Language Group, Word for Word
Williamsburg ExactLingua

WASHINGTON
Burlington The Language Exchange
Federal Way Languages Translation Services
Lynnwood SinoMetrics International
Mukilteo TransACT
Seattle Academy of Languages, Dynamic Language Center, German Language Services, Japan Pacific Publications, Openworld, Sinometrics
Vancouver Columbia Language Services

WISCONSIN
Fond du Lac Mercury Marine
Little Chute Connecting Cultures
Madison Allegro Translations, Geo Group
Milwaukee Argo Translation, International Communication by Design, International Institute of Wisconsin, Iverson Language Associates
River Falls Sajan
Wauwatosa Language Source
West Allis C.P. Gauger

U.S. GOVERNMENT AGENCIES

All U.S. Government agencies need translation from time to time. The question is when and where. There is no simple way to find out, but persistence does pay off, and if you keep exploring by reading the *Commerce Business Daily* (http://www.cbd-net.com), and by following leads, you will find translation work with the government.

Another way to find out about translation in the government is by locating the companies that have translation contracts with federal agencies. The government can provide this kind of information, and you can contact those companies and offer your services.

A word of warning: most government agencies do not accept unsolicited resumes. However, they do post available positions, which are usually accessible through the voice mail menu when you call them. In addition, you may now find Websites for all the major agencies, as well as useful sites listing job opportunities throughout the entire government (see below).

Visit http://usajobs.opm.gov to check information on availability of jobs in the entire Federal Government and to guide youself through the federal job application process.

The following is a list of federal agencies and some comments about the translation needs of each agency.

Agency for International Development (AID), The Ronald Reagan Building, 1300 Pennsylvania Avenue NW, Washington, D.C., 20523
Phone: (202)712-5043 Website: www.usaid.gov
AID is in charge of the U.S. Foreign Aid program. As such, it works in practically every language. Much of the work is done either in-house or in the target country, but from time to time AID needs translation services, and is worth contacting.

Agriculture, U.S. Department of, 1400 Independence Avenue SW, Washington, DC 20250
Phone: (202)720-4623 (Office of Communications) Website: www.usda.gov
This department, oddly enough, actually offers translation courses. We don't know much about its translation needs, except that there must be some, so feel free to find out for yourself.

Air Force, Department of the, The Pentagon, Washington, DC 20330
Phone: (703)545-6700 Website: www.af.mil
This is a huge organization. Over the years it has done an enormous volume of translation, and was a pioneer in machine translation. The present status is not clear. You can try them, but there is no telling whether you'll find out anything specific. Ask them to send you literature about their language and translation needs.

Army, Department of the, Personnel & Employment Service, 6800 Army Pentagon, Washington, DC 20310-6800
Phone: (703)545-6700 Website: www.army.mil
Like the Air Force, the Army too has done and still does a very large volume of translation. The problem is how to get to the sources, which are spread all over creation. Knowing someone at the Pentagon or at any of the bases helps. You'll need to talk to the procurement people either locally or at the above number.

Central Intelligence Agency (CIA), Central Intelligence Agency, Office of Public Affairs, Washington, D.C. 20505 (mailing address)
Phone: (703)482-0623 Website: www.cia.gov
The CIA hires a good number of translators in a great variety of languages. If interested in a CIA language career, call to inquire about employment. General descriptions of various jobs for language specialists are available on its Website.

Commerce, Department of, 1401 Constitution Avenue NW, Washington, DC 20230 Phone: (202)482-2000 Internet: www.commerce.gov
They have an interesting Japanese program which you may want to inquire about. Otherwise, they translate when they have to. Some Commerce agencies that engage in translation are the Patent and Trademark Office, the International Trade, and the National Technical Information Service.

Congress, Library of (LOC), 101 Independence Avenue SE, Washington, DC 20540 Phone: (202)707-5000 Website: www.loc.gov
The LOC employs full-time translators.

Defense, Department of (DoD), Department of Defense, Washington Headquarters Services, 1155 Defense Pentagon, Washington, D.C. 20301-1155
Phone: (703)604-6219 Website: www.defenselink.mil
Inquire about translation work with DoD agencies at the Defense Supply office at the Pentagon. You may want to stop over there to look at their records. DoD does a great deal of translation.

Drug Enforcement Administration (DEA), Drug Enforcement Administration, Office of Personnel, 2401 Jefferson Davis Highway, Alexandria, VA 22301 Phone: (800)882-9539 Website: www.dea.gov
Ask them about Spanish translation and/or interpreting. They do a great deal of this kind of work.

Education, Department of, 400 Maryland Ave. SW, Washington, DC 20202 Phone: 1-800-872-5327 (general inquiries)

Website: www.ed.gov

Energy, Department of (DOE), 1000 Independence Ave. SW, Washington, DC 20585 Phone: (202)586-9534 (the Energy Library) Website: www.energy.gov
The technical library of the DOE needs translation from time to time, and usually contracts out translation work. Call to inquire.

Environmental Protection Agency (EPA), 1200 Pennsylvania Ave., N.W., Washington, DC 20460 Phone: (202)564-0300
Website: www.epa.gov
The EPA usually contracts out translation work.

Federal Bureau of Investigations (FBI), J. Edgar Hoover Building, 935 Pennsylvania Ave., N.W., Washington, D.C. 20535-0001
Phone: (202)324-3000 (main number) Website: www.fbijobs.gov
The FBI employs full-time translators both at its Washington headquarters and in its field offices. All FBI language employees must be U.S. citizens. (Some exceptions are made for rare or unusual languages; linguists must then be legal resident aliens). Call to inquire. (Ask for the Applicant Coordinator).

Federal Trade Commission (FTC), Human Resources Management Office, Room 723, 600 Pennsylvania Ave. N.W., Washington, DC 20580
Phone: (202)326-2222 Website: www.ftc.gov
The FTC is involved in trade with the newly independent nations of Europe. You may want to find out if they need any translation work in this area.

Foreign Broadcast Information Service (FBIS), PO Box 2604, Washington, DC 20013 Tel. 703/521-5638
Traditionally, FBIS, operating also as JPRS (Joint Publications and Research Service), has provided employment for translators in many languages, and has farmed out translation to hundreds of freelancers. The volume is not what it used to be, but it is still worth inquiring, particularly if you work in languages like Arabic, Farsi, French, German, Russian and many less common languages.

Health and Human Services, Department of (HHS), 200 Independence Ave. SW, Washington, DC 20201
Phone: (202)619-0257 Toll Free: 1-877-696-6775 Website: www.hhs.gov

Housing and Urban Development, Department of (HUD), 451 7th St. SW, Washington, DC 20410 Phone: (202)708-1112
Website: www.hud.gov
HUD maintains a division of Immigrant Services, which involves both print and oral media and utilizes both translators and interpreters.

Immigration and Naturalization Service (INS), 425 I St. NW, Washington, DC 20536 Tel. 202/205-2000 (Vacancies)
Internet: www.uscis.gov
The INS uses the services of interpreters in many languages in all of its court locations in the U.S. Call to inquire about participating in this program.

Information Agency, U.S. (USIA), 301 4th St. SW, Washington, DC 20547 Tel. 202/619-4700
Internet: usia.gov/cgi-bin/AT-ebureausearch.cgi
USIA employs translators, radio announcers and journalists specialized in one or more foreign languages. Call their employment office for more information. They also operate the Voice of America in many languages. It is now becoming part of the U.S. Department of State.

Inter-American Foundation, Personnel Department, 901 N. Stuart St., 10th Floor, Arlington, VA 22203
Phone: (703)306-4301 email: info@iaf.gov Website: www.iaf.gov
May have a need for Spanish translation.

Joint Publications and Research Service, PO Box 2604, Washington, DC 20013
See Foreign Broadcast Information Service.

Justice, Department of (DOJ), 950 Pennsylvania Ave., N.W., Washington, D.C. 20530-0001
Phone: (202)514-2000 e-mail: AskDOJ@usdoj.com Website: www.usdoj.gov
The DOJ is a major source of translation and interpreting. If you are interested in working for this department, you may want to do some research first and find out which agencies of the DOJ have been doing translation lately, and in what languages, and then find out who is doing the work (mostly farmed out) and contact those sources.

Labor, Department of (DOL), 200 Constitution Ave. NW, Washington, DC 20210 Phone: (202)219-6677 (job openings) Internet: www.dol.gov
Two DOL agencies, namely, OSHA (Occupational Safety and Health Agency) and BLS (Bureau of Labor Statistics) have need for translation and interpretation in Spanish and other languages.

National Aeronautics and Space Administration (NASA), 300 E St. SW, Washington, DC 20546 Phone: 1-877-NSSC123 (NASA Shared Services Center) Website: www.nasa.gov
NASA does a very large volume of translating and interpreting, but mostly through its major contractors, like Hewlett Packard, Lockheed, IBM, etc. You can contact NASA for data on those companies, and then contact them and ask to talk to their Small Business office for more information.

National Institutes of Health (NIH), 9000 Rockville Pike, Bethesda, MD 20892 Phone: (301)496-4000 Website: www.nih.gov
The NIH translates medical materials in a variety of languages, mostly through contractors.

National Security Agency (NSA), Fort George G. Meade, MD 20755
Phone: 1-866-672-4473 (recruitment and staffing) Website: www.nsa.gov
NSA employs a large number of language specialists, mainly in the area of cryptography. They have an active recruitment program. Call to inquire.

National Virtual Translation Center, 935 Pennsylvania Ave., N.W., Washington, D.C. 20535 Website: www.nvtc.gov
This organization provides translation services to many different government agencies. Applicants must be U.S. citizens. Applications may only be submitted on-line; see website for more information.

Navy, Department of the, Chief of Information, ATTN: Dept. of the Navy, 1200 Navy Pentagon, Room 4B463, Washington, DC 20350-1200
Phone: (703)545-6700 Internet: www.navy.mil
The Navy as a whole does a large volume of translation. It is difficult, though, to locate the specific sources. If you are a Navy veteran, you have a better chance of getting assignments.

Nuclear Regulatory Commission (NRC), 11555 Rockville Pike, Rockville, MD 20852-2738 Phone: (301)415-7000 Website: www.nrc.gov
The NRC contracts out its translation needs. If interested, find out who their present contractor is and get in touch with them.

Peace Corps, 1111 20th St., N.W., Washington, D.C. 20526
Phone: (800)424-8580 Website: www.peacecorps.gov
The Peace Corps teaches a great many languages, and if you want to get involved in their language program call to inquire.

State, Department of, 2201 C St. NW, Washington, DC 20520
Phone: (202)647-4000 Website: www.state.gov
The State Department employs translators and interpreters, and farms out a great deal of translation and interpreting work. To find out more about it, call the Language Services office and ask for information.

Transportation, Department of (DOT), 400 7th St. SW, Washington, DC 20590 Phone: (202)366-4000 Website: www.dot.gov
DOT does not have ongoing translation needs, but they do a translation project from time to time.

Veterans' Affairs, Department of (VA), 810 Vermont Ave. NW, Washington, DC 20420 Phonr: (202)273-5400 Internet: www.va.gov
The VA may need translation occasionally, especially in Spanish. If you are a veteran you may have a better chance to get assignments.

Voice of America, Language Services, 330 Independence Ave. SW, Washington, DC 20237 Phone: 1-202-619-0909 (job hotline) Website: www.voa.gov

See Information Agency, U.S.

MAJOR ORGANIZATIONS

Inter-American Development Bank
202/623-3450 www.iadb.org
The bank hires French, Spanish and Portuguese translators, mostly translating *into* English, and farms out a great deal of work in these languages.

International Monetary Fund (IMF)
202/623-7000 www.imf.org
The IMF employs translators and farms out translation work on such topics as finance, economic development, economic affairs in Third World countries, banking and insurance.

Organization of American States (OAS)
202/458-3000 www.oas.org
The OAS translates a good volume of Spanish and Portuguese and some French from and into English.

United Nations
212/326-7000 www.un.org
The UN employs a large number of translators and interpreters. If you are interested in a UN career, call their employment office and ask for the job application form, which contains detailed information on their require-ments for employment.

The World Bank Group
202/477-1234 www.worldbank.org
The World Bank employs translators and farms out translation work on such topics as finance, economic development, economic affairs in Third World countries, banking and insurance.

World Health Organization
202/861-3200 www.who.org
Compiles and translates medical data in different languages.

APPENDIX F: THE INTERNET FOR TRANSLATORS

The Uses of the Internet for Translators

The translation field has become increasingly "wired," witnessing a proliferation of sites relating to professional activities, job-hunting, commercial products, and online reference materials for translators. It is not an exaggeration to say that translators do themselves (and potentially their clients) quite a disservice by ignoring the virtual translation community.

This section will introduce you to a selection of highly-regarded and well-maintained sites of use to translators. It assumes basic Web literacy. Of course, the Internet's ever-changing nature guarantees that certain websites will decline or disappear, while new ones will emerge by the time this book becomes available. So please be aware that you will probably have to do some updating of the following information on your own.

Where We Are on the Web

First, let us invite you to Schreiber Publishing's website. Our address: **SchreiberLanguage.com**. Its objective is to provide reference literature, training materials, and useful information for translators.

The Almighty Google

One of the latest verbs in English is "to Google." The incredible reach of **www.google.com** is such that we can no longer live without it. To Google somebody means to type the person's name into the Google website and find out instantly everything (well, almost) there is to know about that person. Which applies not only to people but to everything else under the sun. On Google's homepage you will find a function called Language Tools. It allows you to find words and translate text in several major languages from and into English. As in all machine translation, the rate of accuracy here is much less than 100%, but at least it helps you orient yourself through text and terminology.

Professional Activities

Translators wishing to learn about the state of their profession will benefit from a visit to the American Translators Association's site, **www.atanet.org**. I discuss the ATA in greater detail in the chapter on Translators' Organizations; its Website includes information on the Association's formal activities such as conferences, publications and certification procedures. Even if you are not an ATA member, the site is useful because it can guide you to other translation-related sites.

Another major website of interest to translators is the site of the inter-national umbrella organization of the world's translator associations, the International Federation of Translators, found on **www.fit-ift.org**.

Aquarius, at **www.aquarius.net.** Claims to be "the world's language network." This commercial website lists translation agencies seeking translators and interpreters who, in turn, can post resumes to make their services known. It also links to other translation sites.

More recent websites of this kind are **www.ProZ.com**., which bills itself as "the world's leading enabling and sourcing platform for language professionals," and **TranslatorsCafe.com**, which provides useful fuctions for translators looking for work and resources.

Networking with Other Translators

Translators these days often communicate with one another on the Internet, sharing knowledge, passing on information, checking terminology, or just griping about not being paid on time. It all started with what used to be called "chat rooms," which morphed into various kinds of translations forums located in the U.S. and around the world.

One kind of a forum for translators is the newsgroup: subscribers post messages and receive answers (say, to a specialized translation query). A newsgroup for translators is **http://www.faqs.org/faqs/language/translation-faq/.**

Reference Materials

The Translator's Home Companion at:
www.lai.com/companion.html, provides a great deal of useful information for translators.

The Human Languages Page at:
www.june29.com/IDP provides links to other translation-related sites, including some listed here, and to dictionaries.

Online Dictionary Services

Eurodicautom at:
http://ec.europa.eu/eurodicautom/Controller is a very useful service, Eurodicautom handles European languages such as Spanish, Portuguese, French, German, Italian, English, Danish and Dutch. Includes many specialized dictionaries in non-technical, legal and technical areas. Terms are both translated and defined.

Online Dictionaries at:
www.yourdictionary.com covers a far greater range of languages than the above site. It provides links to dictionaries and translations in many specializations.

Glossaries

There are many mediocre glossaries out there in cyberspace, so use caution with this type of online resource. Here are some of the better ones:

http://www.termisti.refer.org/termisti.htm

U.S. Government agencies provide some very useful glossaries. For example:
www.epa.gov/glossary (for environmental terminology).

Finding Cultural Information

A quick way to access cultural and historical information on other countries is via The Electronic Embassy at
www.embassy.org. This service provides links to embassy and/or United Nations home pages of many nations. Most countries' pages include links to cultural resources such as online newspapers, libraries, and so on. You may have to do some digging to find the information you're after, but if it exists online, you will probably find it by starting here. Also the foreign ministries of various countries are a good source for all sorts of information related to that particular country.

Shopping for Dictionaries

A prime source for dictionaries is: **www.schoenhofs.com**.

Major virtual bookstores also have good selections of dictionaries (see box). Examples:

www.barnesandnoble.com
www.amazon.com
www.borders.com

You may also wish to consult these websites of major dictionary publishers:
Elsevier at **www.elsevier.com**
Routledge at **www.routledge.com**
McGraw-Hill at **www.mcgraw-hill.com**
Schreiber Publishing at **www.SchreiberLanguage.com**

Freelancers can find out about the payment practices of translation agencies. For the most part they are free, but you have to join to be able to use them:

www.paymentpractices.net
www.topica.com/lists/transpayment/
www.tcrlist.com

Quick Order Form

Fax orders: (301) 424-2518. Send this form. Website orders: www.SchreiberLanguage.com

Telephone orders: Call 1(800) 822-3213 x28 (in Maryland: 301-424-7737 x128)

E-mail orders: books@SchreiberPublishing.com.

Mail orders to: Schreiber Publishing, 51 Monroe St.,Ste. 101, Rockville MD 20850 USA

Please send the following books, programs, and/or a free catalogue. I under stand that I may return any of them for a full refund, for any reason, no questions asked:

The Translator's Handbook 6th Revised Edition - The Leading Guide for Translators - $26.95

The Translator's Self-Training Program - includes work sources CD (circle the language/s of your choice):

Spanish French German Japanese Chinese Italian Portuguese Russian Arabic Hebrew - $69.00

The Translator's Self-Training Spanish Medical - $69.00

The Translator's Self-Training Spanish Legal - $69.00

The Translator's Self-Training German Patents - $69.00

The Translator's Self-Training Japanese Patents - $69.00

Multicultural Spanish Dictionary - How Spanish Differs from Country to Country - $24.95

American English Compendium 3rd Rev. Ed. - The "Odds and Ends" of American English - $27.95

Arabic Business Dictionary - $24.95 **Chinese Business Dictionary** - $24.95

French Business Dictionary - Business terms from France and Canada - $24.95

German Business Dictionary - $24.95 **Italian Business Dictionary** - $24.95

Japanese Business Dictionary - $24.95 **Global Business Dictionary** - $27.95

Korean Business Dictionary - $24.95 **Portuguese Business Dictionary** - $24.95

Russian Business Dictionary - $24.95 **Spanish Business Dictionary** - Multicultural Business Spanish - $24.95

Spanish Chemical and Pharmaceutical Glossary - $29.95

Dictionary of Medicine French-English with English-French Glossary - $179.50

Net.Wit.Com - $17.50

Sales tax: Please add 5% sales tax in Maryland

Shipping (est.): $4.50 for the first book and $2.00 for each additional product

International: contact us for shipping rates Order total: ____________

Name: ____________________________________

Address: ____________________________________ City: ____________________

State: ______ Zip: _________ Telephone: ________________ e-mail: ____________________

Payment: __ Credit card: __ Visa __ MasterCard__ American Express___Check ___ Money Order

Card number: _______ __________ ___________ _________ Name on card:____________________

Exp. Date: ___ /____